My
Widening
World

Among the books by
ELIZABETH YATES

My Diary, My World
Silver Lining
The Seventh One
Call It Zest
A Book of Hours
The Road Through Sandwich Notch
Is There a Doctor in the Barn?
The Lady from Vermont
On That Night
The Lighted Heart
Up the Golden Stair
Howard Thurman, Portrait
of a Practical Dreamer
Skeezer, Dog with a Mission
Your Prayers and Mine

FOR YOUNG PEOPLE

Amos Fortune, Free Man
Prudence Crandall, Woman
of Courage
With Pipe, Paddle and Song
Patterns on the Wall
Hue and Cry
Mountain Born
A Place for Peter
We, the People
Carolina's Courage
Sarah Whitcher's Story
Someday You'll Write

My Widening World

by

ELIZABETH YATES

THE WESTMINSTER PRESS

PHILADELPHIA

BOOK DESIGN BY DOROTHY ALDEN SMITH

First edition

Published by The Westminster Press®
Philadelphia, Pennsylvania

PRINTED IN THE UNITED STATES OF AMERICA
9 8 7 6 5 4 3 2 1

Library of Congress Cataloging in Publication Data

Yates, Elizabeth, 1905–
  My widening world.

  Bibliography: p.
  SUMMARY: The journal of a young writer beginning her
career in New York City in the 1920's, climaxed by her
marriage to a young engineer and the beginning of a new
life in England in 1929.
    1. Yates, Elizabeth, 1905–   —Biography—Juvenile
literature. 2. Authors, American—20th century—Biog-
raphy—Juvenile literature. [1. Yates, Elizabeth,
1905–   . 2. Authors, American. 3. New York (N.Y.)—
Social life and customs] I. Title.
PS3547.A745Z473 1983   818'.5209 [B] [92]   82-23713
ISBN 0-664-32702-8

1925

1925

Here I am in New York with every intention of becoming a writer. The apartment Martha found is at 147 East 37th Street, in the shadow and rumble of the Third Avenue El. We share the rent, which is fifty dollars a month, and we'll share the food, so it won't cost us much to live. Martha came down from Buffalo three weeks ago and has her room furnished with things she brought from her home—heavy old family furniture, a Chinese desk, an Italian carved chair, a couch and pillows, a Turkish rug and a Russian samovar. The room is on the front and is all set up as a studio. She's already splashing vivid colors on huge canvases.

My room is in the back, looking out on a small garden. It will be quiet, and I don't need the sun for my work. It's a writer's eyrie, and I have it fixed just the right way for me—a small bed and a big plain table. With a stack of paper, a jam jar filled with pencils, and my typewriter, I'm all set. I have three chairs, like Thoreau in his cabin at Walden: "One for solitude, two for friendship, three for society."

In between our two rooms is a bathroom and a tiny kitchen with a two-burner gas range. We each have our own fireplace. It has taken all this week for me to get settled, finding the furniture I needed and unpacking the things I brought from home.

Home! Just writing that word gives me a twinge. I think about the big house in Buffalo where we lived during the winter, and Hillhurst Farm where the wonderful summers were spent. Those places will always be a part of me, as will the Franklin School. I think of Mother and Father, of Jinny, my brilliant older sister, and of my darling younger brother, Bobby; of Miss Hyde, always there when Mother was away and always there to help Mother; of Maria in the kitchen, and Andy, of Lizzie, of Al in the barn with the horses, and Jim in the garden. I think of Brier, my beloved dog, who isn't much younger than me, and of Bluemouse, my horse. If I think too much, the twinge becomes an ache, but how glad I am for them all.

Tomorrow—that's the challenge! Martha will go to the John Murray Anderson School of Design, where she is studying, and I'll go to *The New York Times* with the letter of introduction that Miss May Martin gave me. It's exciting to be here: an ecstatic, pulsing sensation. I feel ready for great things.

September 30, 1925

Finding a job in New York is like being initiated into a secret society, and the password is *experience*. My letter to the *Times* got me nowhere, as Miss Martin's friend had died two years ago. When I asked

8

to see someone else, the first question asked of me was what experience I had had, and the only answer I could honestly give was, "None." So, that was that. Sitting in Bryant Park and looking at the Help Wanted ads in the paper, I saw one from *The New Yorker* and went to their office; but the help they wanted was to sell subscriptions, and I knew I would not be any good at that; besides, it would not get me anywhere from the standpoint of writing. When I got back to 147, there were two short stories in the mailbox, returned from the magazine I had sent them to only last week. I wondered if an editor had even taken time to read them.

After Martha got home, we made tea, sat by her fire and spent hours talking about my future. She has fantastic ideas and some curious contacts. We both agreed that the important thing for me was to keep as much time as possible for writing, but to do anything to make some money until my stories started selling. She knows a commercial photographer who is always in need of models. Tomorrow I'm going to see him. Martha and I are as different as our tastes and talents, but we have a great bond: we have each achieved freedom to pursue our own lives, and we have been able to keep the respect of our families. It's one thing to be free and another to prove ourselves, and that is going to take time.

—

October 2, 1925

What will the family say when they see a picture of me sitting on a pile of congoleum rugs! But I doubt if they will, because I've never seen any of them reading *The American Magazine*. I made $25 for a morning of posing, and that's a lot. Besides, I'd better get over thinking what people will say about me and get on with what I came to New York to do. An idea for a novel has been burning in me for a long time and now I'll be able to get it written. I'll do whatever I can to tide me over financially and write with all the time that I can command.

October 10, 1925

Mother telephoned to say that Brier had died. "Just old age, dear. He didn't wake up this morning."

I took the night train to Buffalo and we had a little funeral. Al had dug a grave in the orchard and made a box which Bobby and I carried. Jinny joined us. Miss Hyde was there, in the background as always. Maria and Lizzie came from the house, and Andy too. We all wanted to pay our respects. It was the first break in the family circle. Bobby, at fifteen, can't remember a time when Brier wasn't part of the household. Walking back to the house after the ceremony, I felt closer to Mother than ever before. It's like what Miss Hyde once said about death: it makes the ranks of the living draw closer together.

Al brought Bluemouse to the door, saddled and bridled and looking more handsome than ever. "Thought you'd feel better if you did something," he said. It didn't take me long to get into jodhpurs and boots, then off we went down the lane and over the fields. I really let her out and the wind of her splendid speed swept some of the aching away from me. When I got back, Maria and Andy and Lizzie were all having their tea in the kitchen, so I joined them.

I asked Maria to see that lots of leaves went into my cup so Andy could tell my fortune. When the tea was all warm inside me and the leaves were in the bottom of the cup and up one side, I handed the cup to Andy. He studied it for quite a while before he started to read. He always makes a good story, and he often makes it better when he takes the tip of his knife and looks under a leaf, but what he found for me was still a long way off.

"They're there," he said, "all those good things you are after, but they're nowhere near—yet."

In the train going back to New York, I made up a story in my mind about Brier and all that he had meant to our family. Does it take death to help us realize the preciousness, the wonder of life?

October 28, 1925

I've got a fascinating job! It starts November 1, for six weeks (then it will be time for Christmas). I saw the ad in the *Times*—Walking Governess needed to take care of five-year-old boy from 2:30 to 5:30 weekdays. The address was in the 60's, just off Fifth Avenue and not far from Mrs. Ogilvy, but I won't run into her, as she is spending the winter in the south of France. When I presented myself as an applicant, Mrs. Hastings-Jones, a handsome but rather forbidding-looking woman, looked me over as if I was not a person in my own right but a tool that she could use for her own purpose. She said that she was to be away for six weeks and wanted to make certain arrangements for her son for that time. She asked many questions, which I must have answered satisfactorily, for she then told me my duties.

I would come to the apartment at 2:30 and take Master Arnold to Central Park for a walk, staying out as long as the weather permitted, then entertaining him with games or conversation until it was time for his supper, when her housekeeper would take charge of him and I would depart. It sounded intriguing, the $10 a day was beyond my wildest dreams, and I still would have my mornings and evenings free.

November 18, 1925

They say it takes all kinds to make a world, but I don't know what kind Master Arnold is! He is interested in just one thing, and no matter what I do, it is the only thing for him. As soon as we cross Fifth Avenue and get into the Park, he whips a tape measure out of his pocket and measures the girth of the trees. When he says "42 inches" or "64" or "18," it is with great excitement, but he isn't a bit interested in what kind of tree it is he has measured. I show him the ducks on the lake, point out a bird in a tree, start to tell him a story, but he has no interest.

Rainy, raw days are the most difficult, because we have to be inside. He has measured everything that can be measured in the apartment, so he amuses himself by drawing numbers on huge sheets of paper, numbers in every imaginable combination. His father is a stockbroker. Perhaps he hears figures talked about so much that he has to make his own. He will soon know more about money than I would ever care to know, but when will he know anything about Winnie-the-Pooh, or Robin Hood, or Sir Launcelot? I'm not sure that he knows my name, but he knows what I measure around the middle and from my shoulders to the floor.

I look ahead on the calendar to when Mrs. Hastings-Jones will return and my task will be completed, but I still hope every day that by some magic I may be able to open another door for her son. However, I am making lots of money and I'm getting Christmas presents for everyone. Books mostly, they are what I like to give (and get), but for Jinny it will be something for her new home.

December 6, 1925

Again, I turn a page in the book of my life.

Year's End, 1925

This is the last entry this year, but I intend to go on with journal-keeping, noting significant events and keeping an eye on my life.

It was wonderful to be home for Christmas, but I can't let myself dwell on just how wonderful: ten days when there was nothing to do but enjoy everything—people, parties, food, friends. I tell myself that I have work to do and my goal must ever be before me. Father gave me an extraordinary present—a bottle of fifty-year-old port from his cellar. In these prohibition days that is like a crown jewel. "Keep it for special occasions," he said. His eyes had their twinkle, and he patted me on my shoulder as he used to do when I was little. A Special Occasion for me will be the day, and days, and more days when work of mine is accepted for publication.

So here I sit in my eyrie as one year merges into

another. Martha hasn't got back yet from Buffalo, and I'm alone with much to think about. There's a fire in my little fireplace, candles in my two pewter candlesticks. There is warmth and light, and shifting shadows cast by the fire and the candles. The hands of the clock are moving toward midnight. I feel on the edge of something tremendous.

1926

1926

January 21, 1926

Last year at Oaksmere, that boarding school fast fading into memory, there was an exciting experience. Actually there were many, but this one appealed to me. It was the visit made by Mr. Gilbert Simons, an editor on the *New York Sun*. He spoke to us about writing in general and particularly about writing for the press. He read some of our literary efforts, without comment, but he did say that, after we graduated, if any of us were really serious about journalism, he would be glad to talk with us further. I decided to take him up on his offer and wrote a letter to him, reminding him of his visit to Oaksmere and saying that I, for one, was really serious.

Two days later I had an answer from him from the Editorial Department of the *Sun*—

Dear Miss Yates:

If Saturday afternoon is convenient for you we could meet then. If you could meet me at the Biltmore under the clock and go to tea at one of the Peg Woofington places where it is sure to be quiet, I could tell you what I have thought about your career. Will you call me at this office at two o'clock tomorrow afternoon? I should like to show you the plant here.

I feel fluttery with excitement, but I must try to be calm, at least when we meet.

January 30, 1926

I had a charming time with Mr. Simons, but if I learned anything, it was what I don't want to do, and that is work on a newspaper. I want to write words that last, not that change every day. Everything at "the plant" seemed so noisy and fast-moving. Presses were turning out papers that were being loaded on dollies to be taken to trucks to be rushed to newsstands. It was hard to hear what Mr. Simons said as he described procedures to me. It wasn't much better in his office, which was cluttered. There were sheets of paper everywhere, half-opened books, and no order that I could see. I could understand why he wanted to go to tea where it would be quiet.

He is tall and quite good-looking, but very reserved. I suppose he's shy and that made me feel less shy. We talked about me, and he was kind and sympathetic. I showed him two of my poems. He nodded as he read them, but all he said that I can remember was, "You have time and promise." I doubt if we ever meet again.

February 15, 1926

Life is a whirl and just being in New York is exhilarating. People are pouring into our lives—friends from home, from school visiting the city. Everybody introduces somebody else, and there are so many men! At home they were boys, now they are college men. Martha and I go to concerts at Carnegie Hall when we can afford them. Theaters are our passion. We stand outside the scalpers' offices on Broadway and wait to get cut-rate tickets. The plays this year are exciting—some we have seen, some yet to see: Alfred Lunt and Lynn Fontanne are at the Theater Guild, Katherine Cornell is in *The Green Hat*, and there's a marvelous musical, *The Vagabond King*. Eva Le Gallienne as Hedda Gabler was superb, but I think I'm going to like her even better in *The Cherry Orchard. Joan of Arc* is coming soon, and Martha can hardly wait for Norman Bel Geddes' production of *The Miracle.* Sometimes after a play, and excited by it with much to talk about, we walk through the park, or along the river, and often we go down to Chinatown.

When we ask our friends to 147, we always entertain in Martha's room, as she has much more furniture and the wind-up victrola. We make tea on her samovar and then we talk, we really soar the heights in conversation. Sometimes we go down to John's in the Village. He lets in only the people he recognizes through his peephole, but once in, it is good Italian food and a bottle of Chianti. The evening may be just for ourselves or we may be a party.

Martha has some fascinating Russian friends, and I am meeting more people all the time. Whether it's ourselves or several, it's always hilarious. We can easily talk half the night away and walk the other half.

Last week, Martha and I left John's at midnight, then tramped along the wharves until dawn. Mists were rolling in from the river and there was a strange breathless feeling, as if time were standing still. It was so beautiful. I felt perilously near to ecstasy, as if my soul was ready for flight into some vast unknown. Turning away from the river and looking toward the city, we saw gray buildings peering from the mist like dream castles. The river was a slow forgetful rhythm; the lights still burning were neglected stars. Maybe we felt what we were seeing, what we were part of, in different ways, because we didn't say anything. That's the best thing about friendship: you don't have to have words, you feel safe in silence.

More than anything, I want to finish my novel, *Cinema*, and send it to a publisher. I'd like to read it to Martha but I won't. I don't understand her paintings enough to comment on them in any way, and she may feel the same about my work. When it's published I'll give her a copy. What a difference between an artist and a writer! Whatever she does is there for all the world to see, my words must grow within me until the time comes for them to move into the world.

March 24, 1926

Ben took me out last night. He is the brother of one of my friends at Oaksmere, and when he called to make a date, I liked the sound of his voice, and when we met I liked him. He has been out of college three years and is the oldest man I know. He's slightly corpulent but otherwise very nice. He is in the advertising business and is going to design some notepaper for me to use when I write letters to editors. He says it will help sell my stories.

We went to see *The King's Henchman*, but it is so popular that Ben could only get standing room. However, we scarcely realized we were standing, because it was so beautiful, words and music sublimely blended. From there we went to Paul Whiteman's new night club. It was gorgeous, the jazz making me feel all thrilly and melty as syncopation does. When we left, we tramped over to 147, stopping at an Automat on the way for coffee and crullers. We talked a lot, then around 5 A.M. we set out for one of my pet walks—along the East River to the Queensboro Bridge and over it. Before us lay mists and the trembling shades of dawn; behind us the city—a cluttered jumble of beloved rock. We were free and the world was ours. There was laughter in our hearts, beauty everywhere, and no return until long after the milkmen had made their customary rounds.

April 1, 1926

Now Ben has gotten serious. He said last night, "I'd like to marry you tomorrow, but I'll wait all my life for you." I didn't want to hurt him, he really is so decent, a brotherly sort of creature, but I had to say no. I had to tell him that there were other things I must do first. He made it worse when he said, "I'm sure I can make you happy." But that's not what I

21

want—comfortable, respectable happiness. Accomplishment may be lean and spare, but it's what I must see to be true to myself. I couldn't seem to put it in words to him. After he left I worked harder than ever on *Cinema*, for the way to end it has been tumbling around in my head with a terrible insistency.

April 2, 1926

It's Good Friday. Martha and I wanted to hear *Parsifal* at the Met, though there were no tickets to be had, only standing room. It was so glorious that we never even knew we were standing for almost five hours. After that we went to an Alice Foote MacDougal's and treated ourselves to waffles and coffee. The music and the settings meant most to Martha, the mysticism of the Holy Grail to me. That's the way it is: we complement and enrich each other.

April 10, 1926

Oh, woe! The novel that began so well and then rushed to its conclusion now seems no good at all. I might be holding ashes in my hands as those pages with their many words. I can't write and I can't give up writing. What am I to do? Some days I feel full of poems, some days of prayers, but most days now I feel full of futility. It's as if I were alone in the universe with all doors shut. Happiness seems like a dream, reality is my despair. It would be so easy to slip in front of a bus on Fifth Avenue and end it all, but I know that would solve nothing.

In my worst moments I seek sanctuary in St. Patrick's and I can generally come away feeling better; a few blocks down the Avenue is the Public Library and that, too, is a kind of sanctuary. So I go back to my eyrie with more resolve. When there's an envelope in my mailbox with a short story returned, I need what sanctuary gives me. It is quite hard not to be discouraged. When will things begin to come my way? I have so many thoughts, so much to say, but there are times when the old fire just isn't there. A little success, just a tiny bit, would fan the flame. Is the fire apt to go out? But I have done one thing: *Cinema* is finished and I shall send it to a publisher.

April 25, 1926

Seward was a senior at Williams last year and now he's in a broker's office in Wall Street. He is sandy-haired, freckle-faced, and fun. We walked in Central Park this afternoon. How prosaic that sounds, but it wasn't. The air had spring in it, streaming sunshine, singing wind, and we felt intoxicated with the joy of living. The world was at our fingertips. We sang and laughed and raced each other. Seward is often shy and quiet, but we do have good times together. I hope he won't get serious, because I don't want things to change yet. It would be so easy to go that route. Maybe the only thing that really matters in life is the human equation: some he and some me. I suppose the propagation of the human race is important and that means marriage, but maybe it isn't for everyone. There just may be some people for whom the propagation of ideas— words, sound, color, form—is important. Maybe I'll never marry.

I wanted to tell Seward my news—that I had

finished my novel, finished it to the extent that my typing was completed, that the manuscript was wrapped up and ready to be put in the mail tomorrow, but I didn't tell him. The feeling of accomplishment was as vibrant in me as the springness of the day was vibrant around us, but I didn't say anything. I thought he might not understand what this meant to me, or that he might not care.

April 26, 1926

Cinema has gone to Little, Brown, in Boston.

May 25, 1926

Today I received a letter from Little, Brown, and a package.

> Dear Madam:
> Your manuscript, *Cinema*, has now been carefully considered and we are very sorry that our readers do not find it exactly suited to our needs at the present time. Also, it is rather too slight for a full-length book.
> We can do nothing, therefore, but return your material and it is enclosed herewith. We assure you that we greatly appreciate your courtesy in permitting us to consider your work and only regret that our decision must be an unfavorable one.

There was another letter in the mail, from Camp Kinni Kinnic, asking me if I would return for "a summer of equitation"—same salary, same duties as last year. I've read that when one door closes another opens. We'll keep the apartment, and Martha will use my room to sleep in. It will be cooler.

June 28, 1926

Before leaving for camp in Vermont, I had a final fling with Cleve. It's almost like family, being with him, because I've known him so long. He's a college friend of one of my older brothers and has visited at the farm. He treated me then like somebody's little sister, but he seems to have a different kind of interest in me now that I'm on my own and making my way in New York. He writes poetry and does book reviewing. His poems are more sophisticated than mine, but they get published. If I can stand his being so superior with me, I think I can learn things from him that will help me.

He took me to dinner at Longchamps, then to the theater to see Jane Cowl. We didn't go dancing, but went back to the apartment, because Cleve wanted to read me some of his poems. I liked them, though I didn't always understand them. Everything seemed right for me to read him a short story that I had just finished and want to send out before I leave for Vermont. He listened, and maybe that proves something, for Ben falls asleep when I read to him. After the last page he said, "I'd call you a second Katherine Mansfield."

"But I want to be a first myself."

He started to get sprawly and that made me mad, much as I like him.

"Come on, this is what life is all about, not words on paper."

"No, it isn't, not yet anyway."

End of Summer, 1926

The work has been good, in the saddle all day, many an evening idling on the lake in a canoe with one of the other counselors. As it's my second year, I've been given more freedom and more responsibility. Except for the Sabbath Sermon and editing the camp paper, there's been no time for writing, but I've jotted ideas down in my notebook, and I'll have plenty to work on and with next winter. It's my fallow time and perhaps that's as good for a mind now and then as it is for a field. I've made many new friends and it seems they'll all be turning up in New York to see me and meet Martha.

From camp I went to Hillhurst Farm to be with the family for a while. The whole way of life there is so beautiful, so ordered, so full that I could almost succumb to it, but I won't. I go along with it, marveling that my old rebellion at the social aspect of the days has faded somewhat. Ben came for a week. The family all like him and hope "something will come of it"; but I find his attention boring. Jinny came out to the farm several times and she positively shines with all she is doing—active in every kind of society event, especially ones that aid charities, winning tennis matches, and talking of horse shows, but not this year. She's getting plump in the middle and that makes Mother look at her adoringly. It must be wonderful to lead the kind of life that pleases the people near you who know you and love you. I may never do that. They may not be pleased with what I do, but I hope that someday they'll be proud of me.

Bobby and I had some long rides together and

we talked. He wanted to know all about New York, and, even though I haven't anything to show for my time there, he was interested, maybe not so much in what I am doing as in me. He's beginning to chafe at restrictions: what he'd like to do versus what Father has in mind for him to do. I tried to tell him that he was so young, that he hadn't even finished school yet, then I remembered people used to say that to me. He's so dear; he would never ride roughshod the way I seemed to have to do, but he has an aching need to be recognized for himself.

Life seems to play a kind of hide-and-seek with us, especially when we're growing up. With each of us, our deepest need is to be found, but we continue to feel lost. Whenever we got to a place in our conversation where I thought I might be able to say something to Bobby that would be helpful, he would say, "Come on, let's give them a run," and off we'd canter.

I'm trying to work out something in my mind. We're clay, of course, but not in the hands of another, rather in the forces of life. Clay is molded, wood is shaped, stone is cut, silver refined, but a human being is shaped by influences, forces, tensions. Maybe, and this is a thought that startles me, when we begin to find ourselves we begin to find God. Our search for identity, then, is twofold.

September 10, 1926

New York again, and while life at Hillhurst was satisfying, the city is stimulating. Something in me quickens at possibility. Tomorrow I begin the round of job hunting. It's hard, because often it seems there is so little that I can do, but I must fight off discouragement with all the power that's in me. It's devastating to get discouraged. It breaks down the thin walls of strength within me that have taken so long to build.

September 15, 1926

An intriguing ad took me to the employment office of R. H. Macy, and now I'm one of their corps of Comparison Shoppers. I think it is going to be exciting and very good training for me as a writer. It will call upon all of me and involve my senses totally. We will meet early in the morning, before the store officially opens, and we will be given our instructions for the day. If Gimbel's or Bloomingdale's or some other department store has merchandise similar to Macy's, our job is to see that particular item and report back on it. It may be a fur coat, a refrigerator, or anything at all, but since Macy's policy is to sell 6 percent below its competitors, we have to see the product, study it, and bring back a complete report, then the decision will be made by Macy's to reduce its price or keep it.

The first day I was sent over to Newark to compare a stove being advertised with Macy's model. I felt like a spy. It was delicious, looking over, into, around, under the stove, remembering its features, every least detail, then going off and writing down a complete report. It's good for observation, memory, right use of words, all that a writer needs. It will help me, and I'm being paid very well with all my expenses—travel, luncheon, and anything out-of-pocket. The important thing is never to get caught, or reveal the reason for the intensity of my interest.

October 10, 1926

We've added to our household! Today when we took our glass milk bottles back to the delicatessen store on Third Avenue to get our nickels for them, we were given a free black kitten. At first we called him Soot, but we soon changed his name to De Profundis. We've been reading and talking about Oscar Wilde lately and that name seemed more appropriate. He's lively and delights in teasing us, messing himself up in Martha's paints, then scampering into my room. He likes to investigate my typewriter. Watching him, I feel there are times when he might write better stories than I do, except that I don't write on the typewriter. A pencil traveling over lined paper is my method. When I have the work as I want it to be, then I type my finished copy. Each story may be what I want it to be, but it doesn't seem to be what an editor wants. Three have just come back in the mail. One rejection slip said, "Try us again." I will.

I'm taking a philosophy course at New York University on Wednesday evenings and it's a great mind opener. The lectures are good, and the books given us to study are challenging, but often my old trouble comes back: wandering! I find myself thinking about the elderly man in the front row, making up a story about him instead of listening to the professor. That's my problem—everything is a story to me. My head teems with ideas. I get excited, and, once back at 147, stay up the rest of the night writing. Martha says that if her luxury is paint, mine is candles. I like to write by candlelight. It's soft, and

29

there's a feeling that the thoughts eluding me may be lurking in the shadows. I've finished two new stories and sent them to magazines.

November 10, 1926

The stories have come back. What is wrong with me? I saw an ad in the paper for a Literary Adviser. Her name is Miss Weil and she lives in Newark. I made an appointment to see her on a day when Macy's gave me an assignment in New Jersey, and I asked for an extra hour, which Macy's allowed me. From the moment I walked into her room, I wished I had not come. It was all so untidy. She wanted me to leave the stories and asked me to return in a week. I said I couldn't be sure of being in Newark next week and would prefer to wait. So she turned the pages of the two stories, made an occasional comment, read the poem without comment, shuffled the pages together and handed them back to me. She said she had no particular advice to give me, that the stories were good and I should work harder.

"But I'm not getting any accepted."

"Acceptance comes in time. Keep sending them out to the different magazine markets."

"What advice do you have for me?"

"I've given you it—work harder."

So I paid $10 to be told what I already knew.

On the way back to New York, my thoughts were of Miss Albertina Russell, my wonderful tutor during the year at Oaksmere. She did not give me advice so much as counsel, and there is a world of difference between those two words.

December 6, 1926

I'm twenty-one now. I can vote.

December 20, 1926

We're going home for Christmas, and De Profundis will travel in a hatbox and Martha will have him with her in her berth. I'll have to give up Macy's and take my chance at finding an equally good or better job when I get back. I've loved the work. It's been exhausting physically, but otherwise stimulating, and I feel as if I had broken out of the terrible wheel of futility. Many times my boss has said, "Your reports are well written . . . extremely well . . . amazingly well." One day the comment was, "You're wasted in a job like this. Have you ever thought of being a writer?"

1927

1927

January 1, 1927

That last night home was a story in itself! After dinner we were all in the living room by the fire. Father settled behind his paper. I picked up a book, but didn't really feel like losing myself in it. The warmth of Christmas was all around, and the knowledge that I would soon be going my separate way made it seem warmer than ever. I must have got caught up in my book, because, before I knew it, the others had drifted from the room and I was alone with Father. The newspaper rattled, then was folded and laid on the table. He wants an accounting, I thought. A businessman always wants that.

"You like what you **are** doing in New York?"

"Yes. Of course. Very much."

"But what are you doing?"

"I've had some interesting jobs, most of them temporary. Made lots of friends. Gone to the theater and concerts. Had lots of fun."

"You went away to become a writer."

"Yes."

"And what does that mean?"

"I've written one novel."

He didn't look in the least interested, but why should he? He never reads novels.

"Will it be successful?"

I shook my head. "Not yet." How could I tell him of the letter I had received from Little, Brown? "I think I will do better with my next novel." Words hid my heartache but not my hope.

"That was a nice young man who came up to see you when you were home last summer."

"Oh, Ben? Yes, he's a very decent sort of person."

"Anything serious?"

"No." I felt silenced. The respectability of marriage, that's what they want for me, I thought.

His hands were reaching for the newspaper. "Well, you are doing what you want to do." Then he settled back into *The Wall Street Journal*.

I'm doing what I have to do, I wanted to say, but couldn't get the words out.

I picked up the book I'd been reading, but it didn't seem to have any more appeal to me, so I left and went up to my room—disgusted with myself because I couldn't seem to explain to Father what I felt, and hurt because when everything here seems so wonderful on the surface the atmosphere of disapproval makes me feel like a stranger. In their eyes my life is going for nothing, but I've got to keep on, and even if it takes me years, I know that my work will prove itself—and me—someday.

Now that I've written all this down I feel better. And that's the way it has always been, the way it will be. I make an entry in my journal, I write a poem or a story, and I feel relieved. When it's out of me and onto paper, I can see the thoughts for what they are. Or may become.

I stretch out my hands to the new year. What will it bring? What will I bring to it? During these hours between midnight and morning, I've replaced the candles and the fire has gone out; but light is beginning to creep into the room and there's a fire in me: to do, to accomplish.

January 27, 1927

I never thought to be a saleslady, but that's what I am, and loving it! The Frankl Gallery is on East 48th Street, so it's an easy walk from the apartment. They have fabrics, small furniture, china, and things that are a joy to handle because they are so beautiful. The customers can be delightful or annoying, but each one must be treated like royalty. The people I work with are such fun, especially Mrs. Howard. She has a friend who is an editor on *The American Magazine*, Mildred Harrington. She wants me to meet her.

March 30, 1927

Father took Bobby and me to Bermuda for a week. It was school vacation for Bobby, and Mr. Frankl was willing to give me a week off. The journey out by ship was thrilling, just the three of us, and there didn't seem to be any troublesome talks or painful silences. We enjoyed each other as people. Oh, the warmth of the sun, the singing of birds, the air so fragrant from the fields of Easter lilies, and back of it all the saltness of the sea. One day we cycled to

Elba Beach and spent hours on the pink coral sand or jousting with the surf, then enjoyed a picnic basket packed by the hotel. We were drenched with sunlight, brimful of happiness. And to think that these sands, this water, sunrays and sea winds are mine forever because I've been a part of them and can tuck them away in my mind to relive.

April 17, 1927

Martha had a party tonight, an Easter celebration. There were lots of people, mostly her friends, but friends brought friends, so sometimes we didn't know who different people were, but we knew we were having a good time. The doorbell rang.

"That'll be Bill," Martha said, "we sent him out to get some ice."

I was the nearest one to the door, so I went to open it.

"I'm Bill."

He had the nicest smile and the warmest voice, and his eyes were gray. Had I ever really looked into a man's eyes before? During the evening we were often together, accidentally, in the crush of people in the room that seemed much too small, then deliberately as we found so many things to talk about. Before he left we made a date to go on a hike next Saturday in the Highlands of the Hudson.

April 23, 1927

We took the train to Haverstraw, walked three miles to Tompkins Cove, then followed an Indian trail over the Timp Range back into the Catskills. We were the first over the trail this year and it was gone in many places. Often we lost ourselves. It took thinking and fighting through the brush to find ourselves again. We rested where the sun shone warm on the rocks. We found a spring near which cowslips were growing in golden clumps. We climbed Timp—1,100 feet; and Bockberg—1,500. They were steep, but there were stubby trees to catch hold of. We stood on the summits and saw for miles and miles great rolling seas of russet and green mountains with touches of dogwood coming into bloom among the trees.

When we found the perfect place, Bill made a small fire and we cooked our meal over it—warming a tin of beans and making a pot of coffee. There was a comfortable cranny against a rock wall, and there we stretched ourselves out, the earth firm beneath and the sky so blue above. The valley was far below us and beyond were distant hills. I had *The Gypsy Trail* in a pocket of my rucksack, and I took it out and read some of my favorite poems to Bill. When I told Bill that I wanted to write, he was interested; he even asked if I would read some of my work to him sometime.

When we came down the trail and out of the woods, the setting sun had turned the river to scarlet with cloud reflections, and a star could be seen over a ridge. The birds were singing their last songs. It was late when we got back to the city. We had laughed and talked and been a part of beauty all through a day. I felt strong, as if nothing could ever hurt me. I think this has been the most exhilarating day of my life. The strength of nature seemed to flood through my feet and up out my fingertips. I don't know when we'll meet again. Somehow it doesn't matter. Bill travels a lot for his company and is in New York only for brief times. He said he would telephone me and we would make another date.

May 10, 1927

Jean came down from Smith College for the weekend and it was good to see her, someone with whom I can keep the link forged in childhood. We drank many cups of tea and we talked about everything—work, our families, books, people, God. She says I'm like a wellspring, sensitive and serious. I showed her the copybook in which I've written my poems, and she read them slowly, often commenting, not like a teacher but a friend. She said she could see in my words and their rhythm the kind of life I was living. We fell into long silences, and our talk was never meaningless.

"You have a commitment to goodness, to beauty," she said, "don't sacrifice it just because you feel you must sell."

While I was pondering her words, she said something else that made me think. "And don't be unwilling to write something tart and caustic. Life has that side, too."

July 5, 1927

A poem of mine has been published in the *New York World!* I submitted it two weeks ago with a stamped, self-addressed envelope enclosed, and it didn't come back to me. It is in "The Conning Tower," a column that appears daily in the paper and is read by everyone. Franklin P. Adams is the columnist, and he keeps as pleasing a balance between prose and verse as he does between his own work and that of others. He is said to have an eye out for new writers, and I'm certainly that on the Literary Scene! One poem out of a year of work, but what a place for it! It means that F.P.A. has recognized me and maybe other editors will, too. Some people may be in the *Blue Book* or the *Social Register*, but I am in "The Conning Tower"!

July 20, 1927

Martha is going to Paris for a year to study, so we are packing up the apartment and I've found a much smaller one at 243 East 36th Street. We've had great times and gained a lot from each other, but probably it's good for us to go our own ways now. "He travels the fastest who travels alone," Kipling says. I want to spend all my spare time on weekends and in the evenings working on my novel, *Clothed with the Sun*. More than anything, it must be finished. It is filled with things I want to say, thoughts I want to give to the world, and somehow writing it helps me to justify my life.

August 15, 1927

An article I did about Bermuda was bought by *The Smokers' Companion*. It was exciting to see my name in print, to receive a check for $25, but best of all was the letter that offered me a job on the magazine. It won't be hard to give up my work at the

Frankl Gallery, because this is a real step forward in my chosen world of writing.

Now that the novel is finished and on its way to a publisher, I'll take a couple of weeks off before I begin the new job. I hope something will come of *Clothed with the Sun*. In any case, I'm glad it's written. My head is cleared of those ideas, and I'm ready for more.

Bill gave me a book by Glenn Frank, *Fishers of Men*. In it I read, "Sure as the tide goes out and then comes in again, just so will all we give out come back to us."

End of Summer, 1927

Two weeks at Hillhurst are a beatitude after the hot days in New York. So much is the same, but Bobby isn't here. He's in the Canadian wheatfields, working as a harvester and having tremendous adventures. Jinny is busy with her family, but Bluemouse is still the best horse in the world to ride, and Andy can still find a fortune in a teacup. Yesterday when he read mine he pushed a leaf aside to discover another leaf. "That's a man in a business suit," he said.

"Oh, Andy, it's just another tea leaf."

"There's tea leaves and tea leaves," he answered, "but there's only one looks like that man. He's so close to you that I can't tell for sure whether he is now, or will be, your man."

Maria started to fill my cup again, but I didn't want to drink any more tea. I had fortune enough for one day.

Here I am back in New York, settled in at 243 East 36th, reveling in solitude but no longer alone, because I brought a puppy back with me—a Sealyham, Sinna Lezah, and I'm sure he is going to be a dog of character as well as a staunch companion.

As Chief Manuscript Reader at *The Smokers' Companion* I am wildly happy. This is my work, my life. The very smell of the paste, the clip of scissors, the click of typewriters are thrilling to me. I can work tirelessly, and the great thing is that I am in the office only mornings. Most of my work can be done at home, so I don't have to leave Sinna for too long a time. I feel that now I am really started, I've been given a chance to prove myself and I will forge ahead.

Everyland Magazine has accepted a story of mine, but the novel has been returned. I've put it in my bottom drawer with *Cinema.* Yesterday when I was having luncheon with Mildred Harrington, I told her about the novel. I had to tell somebody, because I was so disheartened. She cheered me when she said, "Of course you can and will do things! What is more, you have already done things."

"So few. So little."

"You must remember that in giving you the wonderful gift of verse, the good Lord also endowed you with the capacity for exquisite suffering. That's why discouragement hurts."

"But it's taking me so long to get anywhere."

"Things will break eventually. They do for those who keep faith with themselves, and you are doing that."

October 10, 1927

Bill is in New York for a whole week. We had
dinner last night at John's and it was warm enough to
sit in the garden. We had bowls of ravioli and a bottle
of Chianti. Just to look into his warm, smiling eyes, to
listen to the tone of his wise-worded voice, made up
for all my recent disappointments. We talk about
everything, books and plays and events in the world,
but we always seem to end up talking about God. I'm
still searching for some reality, which I think Bill has
found. He tells me about his work and I tell him
about mine. When he looks across the table at me his
eyes say he believes in me.

Later

Saturday morning early we were on the first train
out of the city. We got on the Timp trail by nine and
Sinna was in his element, frolicking around us,
rolling in the leaves, rushing off on some excitement,
then dashing back and not quite sure to whom he
should show his affection first. Last time we came
this way, the woods were alive with the thrust of
spring; now the green is tired and there are dried
leaves to scuff through.

Whenever we found an opening in the forest, we
could see flashes of color on the distant hills—copper
and scarlet and gold. Sinna began to weary after a
few miles, so we shifted some of the things from Bill's
pack into mine, and Bill gave him a ride on his back.
As soon as we reached our first real height—hot and
tired but exhilarated—I flattened out on the sun-

warmed rock and, with my arms outstretched, let the sun caress me as the ground held me. Bill asked me what I was thinking. I said I wasn't thinking, I was praying.

"Oh, Earth, flood through me with your great strength—the strength that rears trees into mansions for the winds and sends rivers leaping to the sea."

"Sounds like a poem."

"It will be—my Antaeus poem."

Later we followed a trail down to a small lake. Bill found the right place to make a fire. We broiled steaks, boiled coffee, ate bread and apples. Sinna had his share, too. Then we studied our map and discovered that a woodland road could get us to Arden for a late train back to the city. Darkness overtook us long before we reached the station, but there were stars. The mountains were a dim rim against the night, the grass was dew-soaked, and Sinna, riding in the pack on Bill's shoulders, was asleep.

"We've come a long way," Bill said.

October 20, 1927

Cleve wanted to see me, so I suggested we go out to dinner. I was afraid he might get slushy if we stayed at the apartment. He's thinking more of me since another poem of mine has been in the *Herald Tribune*. He writes for the *Saturday Review* and has actually mentioned me in his column. He asked if I wanted to see what he had written.

"You read it to me."

"In these first poems there is an honesty of emotion and a directness of expression that make the work worthy of attention. They are youthful poems,

45

filled with revolt against the world as it unfolds itself to the author. But even when she is repeating sentiments which are too familiar to us, her intensity of feeling carries us with her. She does have something to say and she says it at any cost to poetic structure. Her future work will bear watching."

There wasn't anything I could say for a long time. Then the words I wanted came to me. "Cleve, for one whose bread has been rejection slips, this is heady wine."

November 5, 1927

Mildred thinks I should show my short stories to someone capable of judging them rather than sending them out, as I've been doing, and in most cases getting them back. She suggested Loyola Sanford, not so much as an agent but as a person who represents authors that appeal to her. In preparation for meeting her next week, I've spent this evening going over the stories and trying to decide which ones merit her time. The El rumbles on through the night, Sinna makes whiffling sounds in his sleep, and I read—sometimes with satisfaction, more often with dismay. Why do I use such fancy words? Why do I persist in writing about things beyond my ken?

Here they are, spread out on the table before me. Some were written as many as three years ago; all have been sent out several times. *Tabloid Serial*— that's about three wives, each one in a different type of setting; the words are all right, but I can see now that there is no story line to keep it moving. *Streak of White*—that's about an elderly dressmaker who wanted love and never found it. *Ties and Tigers*—how

46

did I dare to set a story in India and inject into it a grisly murder? *Lunatic at Large*—on that one an editor wrote "not sufficient characterization." *Le Rouge Gagne*—gambling at Monte Carlo, and I think I must have wanted to show off my French. *News Item*—about a suicide, and I always thought it was one of the best. *Fools in Darkness*—a tale of mixed-up lovers. *Three Steps*—what did I know about the inner thinking of a prostitute? *Leaves from a Notebook*—marrying without love, a favorite subject of mine and the brunt of my second novel. *Blonde Etching*—mystery, murder, suicide, market crash, domestic troubles; no wonder it came back to me! The two most recently done still please me—*Touching Finger Tips*, about a day in the country, and *The House of Loving Touch*. In each one, the conversation sounds not as if I were making it up, but as if I were really listening to, or overhearing, two people very much in love. Which ones shall I show to the unknown Loyola?

Our first meeting was in her office, a room of her apartment in the Village. I thought I was going to feel scared, but I didn't. The room was small, with a flat desk, a few neat piles of manuscripts, and a bowl of apples, one of which she offered me. There were many books and just two chairs. Whatever visitor she has must feel rather special. She is tall, slender, quiet; her dark hair is drawn back into a simple knot, and her dark dress is of no particular style. Her very plainness is her beauty. She looked at me as if she really saw me, and she asked questions that were easy for me to answer. I had a portfolio with six of my best stories in it, and when I handed it to her, she took it as carefully as if I were giving her something

47

very precious. We agreed to meet in a week's time.

"And talk," she said, with a smile that made me feel I was with the right person.

At our second meeting, she came to my apartment for supper, and we did talk then, half the night. This time I was the listener, for she had much to tell me.

I told her that I thought I wasn't getting anywhere, and she countered by telling me that in my various jobs I had been observing life on many levels.

"Model, governess, comparison shopper, saleslady, teacher at summer camps, magazine editing—they all have had bearing on writing. It's a course you've given yourself, and you've been paid for what most people have to pay for. Your senses are your tools, and these varied experiences have been sharpening your tools."

I put my hand on the pile of stories and said, "These represent years of work."

"And all the time you have been building into yourself something called discipline. You've finished tasks you set yourself, and you rose out of disappointment. Three years? That's not so long when you measure it up to a life."

"Do you think you can sell any of my stories?"

"I have no doubt, perhaps not these, but the ones you will write."

After she left, I went on thinking. She was giving me encouragement as Miss Russell had when I worked with her, yet each one made it clear that I would have to go on, keep on, if achievement was to be mine. Is life ever going to be long enough for me to learn all that I have to learn?

Thanksgiving, 1927

Was there ever such a day or such a dinner! Bobby is back from the wheatfields looking stalwart and handsome. He is overflowing with stories of his adventure, and he has a magnificent big dog with him, Ronno. Mother and Father, Bobby and Ronno, are all staying at the Commodore and that's where we had dinner. It was fun to be a small family, because so often at home it's a big family, and it gets bigger as the older ones marry and add to it. Father wants Bobby to learn the hotel business, and he'll be starting in at the kitchen in the Commodore, so we'll be able to see each other often.

Bobby told us of his adventures—the hard work, the way he had put his boxing experience to good use, and then about how Ronno had saved his life. It was like reading a book or going to a play just to listen to him, but it was all real, and it was my little brother who was the chief actor. Little? He's taller than I am, and he says I'm not to call him Bobby anymore, but Bob.

Late in the afternoon he walked back to 243 with me. Sinna took to Ronno immediately, and it was fun to watch how gentle the big dog was with the little one. Like Bob, I thought, always doing nice things for people. I put the kettle on to make tea, because I didn't want Bob to go. I wanted to hold on to him, keep him talking about his time in the northwest, fill my eyes with the sight of him and my ears with the sound of his voice.

He pulled some papers out of his pocket. They were in his handwriting.

49

"It was four days coming home on the train, and I spent some of the time scribbling down my experiences. Thought you might like to read them."

I took them from him. There were forty pages in all, written in pencil on both sides of the paper. His handwriting was never the best, and the motion of the train didn't help, but glancing through the pages, I felt that they positively sang with the reality of what he had been through, what he had done.

We talked far into the night. He wants me to help him make the pages into a book.

"Will you have the time?"

"Oh, Bob, that's one of the advantages of being a writer, I can control my time, work in the day, write at night. But you'll be busy down in that big kitchen at the Commodore. Will you have time to talk with me more, because I'll have lots of questions to ask you, and it will take more than these pages to make a book."

Bob had the kind of smile that could say more than words.

After he and Ronno left, I took Sinna for a walk through the dark, quiet streets. I wanted to think about the adventure I would be on, using Bob's forty handwritten pages. Now I'm sitting by my little fire, still thinking. There is so much I'll have to know to give background to the story and to expand it.

December 20, 1927

I do have time, plenty of time. This week the office staff of *The Smokers' Companion* were informed that the magazine was going out of business and that the issue we were working on was the last one.

Somehow I'm not sorry. There will be hours and days, maybe months, to work on Bob's book, and I've a chance to do an article for *The American Magazine*. Mildred said if they liked it, it could lead to more articles.

It may not be possible for me to explain it to anyone else but I can to myself—what I am doing right now is serving an apprenticeship. Seeing my time that way makes me feel like a craftsman of old, working under a master and slowly perfecting the necessary skills. Who is my master? The great ones of English prose, of course, but in the long run it is myself. I go back to what Miss Russell said to me, "Please yourself." The trouble is that I get harder and harder to please, but maybe that is a good thing.

New Year's Eve, 1927

I end the year with a big decision: from now on I am going to sign my work Brett Yates. That is strong-sounding, much more so than Betty, and I hope to do work that will match up to it. Just as I had to get away from Buffalo to find myself in New York, so I have to get away from the person I've been to the one I have every intention of being. What's in a name? More than the sound: a clarion call.

1928

1928

A March day that feels like spring.

So much has been happening! I had just started planning Bob's book with him when Mildred called to say that the *American* had accepted my article and that there was a part-time job in the Research Department if I cared to apply for it. Of course I applied the very next day and was given the job. I can do it on my own time, working mostly at the Public Library to gain background information required. It has to do with particular people who have been successful in their lives, often against great odds. These success stories are wonderful. They show the maintenance of single purpose, one objective dominating the mind. Muddled minds never go far. Life has been hard for most of these people, and that is why they forced themselves to forge ahead and hew out their work and so make their names.

When I have finished one assignment for the *American* I can then turn to Saskatchewan and wheat harvesting to learn about all the things that will give background and a sense of place to Bob's story. In both cases, reading and note-taking are done at the library; my actual writing can be done at home. I told Bob I wasn't going to do anything to add to the details about boxing. That was all his and no words of mine were needed. It's too gory for me. In the evening, after I finish my reports for the *American*, I type up Bob's material for the next time we get together.

Ronno is staying on a farm in Mountainville, across the Hudson, and Bob goes over there weekends to be with him. Sometimes I join him with Sinna, and the dogs have as much fun as we do. They romp and wrestle with each other while we walk and wrestle with words. My problem is that every time Bob and I meet to discuss the book, he remembers more things that happened and wants me to fit them in.

April 12, 1928

Seven Sons, the story that *Everyland Magazine* accepted last fall, has just appeared. It's actually in print, with my name in print just a little smaller than the title. They sent me two copies of the magazine and a check for $25. A letter from the editor said that it was different from anything they have had, but it carried their message. *Everyland* is published in Boston and it is a magazine of world friendship for boys and girls. The story is as Irish as I could make it, and, when I was writing it, it seemed as if the stories Lizzie used to tell when I was little came back to me. The words lilted as I read them in print and gave me a feeling of being in another world. I sent the extra copy home to Mother, hoping she would enjoy it. Her roots are Irish, and one of our heirlooms is a sampler done by her great-great-grandmother, Eleanor Obeirne, when she was thirteen years old in Ireland.

April 15, 1928

Two letters in my mailbox: one from Mother saying my story filled her with wonder and surprise, "I'm proud of you." The other was from Miss Hyde, "It is a true gift you have been given, and you deserve great praise for the way you are developing your talent." Lovely words; I have framed them in my heart.

April 17, 1928

Bill and I went to John's last night to celebrate the fact that we have known each other for exactly one year. We ate in the garden, and the air was so still that the candle on our table hardly flickered at all. We always have more to talk about than will fit into the time and we often get very philosophical. Bill knows so much more than I do. After all, he's been in the world seventeen years longer than I have and what he knows he is sure of. I'm still searching. I tell him about the different churches I've been going to ever since I've been in New York.

The most unusual was a Russian church Martha took me to, where we stood around, held lighted candles, understood nothing, but savored the atmosphere. I've been to a Jewish synagogue, a Baptist revival, ever so many churches, and often to St.

Patrick's or St. Thomas's on Fifth Avenue, for there are times when the music, the fragrance of incense, and the beauty of light through stained-glass windows seem to answer my need. I wonder where and what God is and I come back to answering my own question: as with writing, I have to find the way myself for God to have meaning in my life. So we talk a lot about God. Bill doesn't try to divert me, or direct me, or improve me. He listens, then says something that makes me go into myself to reply.

Tonight I asked Bill if he thought I was an atheist.

"What did you think when we stood on Timp just a year ago and saw all those billowing ranges around us and above us the sky?"

"I think—I think I felt face-to-face with God."

"And where were you?"

"There, too."

Then I saw something so clearly that I wrote it on a piece of paper and handed it to Bill. Am I an atheist? An atheist is one who does not believe in himself. I do believe in myself. Therefore I am not an atheist.

"Look, I've made a theorem, and I was never good with algebra when I was at the Franklin School."

"Don't worry about algebra if you make a Q.E.D. with your life."

Then he asked me if I had finished my Antaeus poem.

"Bill, that was way back in October—to think that you remembered!"

"You didn't forget, did you?"

"No."

"Can you say it to me?"

"I'll try—some of it anyway: 'Antaeus wishing to renew his strength / Embraced the earth with his body's length . . . Follow Antaeus if you wish to find / Sustenance for your body and mind.' "

"You've skipped some."

"Yes, three verses in the middle. Sometime when it's published I'll send it to you."

"What is its title?"

"*Remedia Natura.*"

When we left, we rode on the top deck of a bus, but we didn't get off at 36th Street. We stayed on, and the bus went to the end of its line, way past Central Park, then turned around. The conductor came up for our fares and Bill gave him another two dimes. The lights of the city were beautiful, the air soft; there was laughter from some people still on the bus, silence from others. With my hand resting in Bill's I felt so safe, so sure.

When we said good-by at the door of my apartment, Bill added his familiar phrase, "And the rest you know." Something in me went still, like a clock losing its tick. I felt afraid. Now, as I write about this evening, what is it I am afraid of?

Before dawn

What does it mean when I say I love
    you?
It means that my heart is in your
    keeping for a while.
I think of no tomorrows or uncertain
    future years,
I see only tonight and the splendor of
    bared hearts.

This is no fragile thing woven of
    moonlight hours,
Rather it is the strength of those who
    know mountains
Brisk with winds, tender with clouds.
I have no bonds to bind your heart to
    mine,
Only hands to offer all my heart to you
With deep-felt thanks, for, due to you,
I have more love for lovely things,
    more pity,
And more hours of loneliness.

Never before have I written a letter in my journal; I do it now because it is a letter that will not be
sent to the one to whom it is addressed.

May 20, 1928

Next best to talking with Bill are his letters to me
when he is away. His flowing handwriting is like the
sound of his voice when he is talking. I see it on an
envelope with my name in my mailbox and my heart
gives a great leap. I keep his letters to reread when
we don't see each other for a time, and the box they
are in is marked Peruvian Notes. I often call him The
Gentleman from Peru because of his far traveling.
Some of the letters are the happy words of friendship,
casual and lively; some are comments on my writing.
These are taken to my heart and mind, for he has
become my mentor above all others.

"The idea is great but it seems too long, too
wordy. It's a Trivia gem if boiled way down. A few of
your sentences convey the idea beautifully, the oth-

ers are repetitious. You are doing real writing. Your growing is evident in your letters. They've changed a lot, same delightful style and insight, but with more body, more action."

There is one written from Boston on a stormy night when he was lonely. "My thoughts constantly turn toward you and I wonder where you are and what you are doing. What fun this night would be were we together! I realize how strong in me is some strange influence that would throttle the expression of thoughts which often seem as vital as life itself. Why is it hard for me to say that I love you dearly, that the attributes I value most I find combined in you—enthusiasm, intelligence, honesty, spontaneity. When I am with you my thoughts—like pigeons released by a loving hand—soar toward the sun, but a silent man walks beside you. I would not possess you for that is death itself, but I pray that the capacity and the opportunity to experience much of life with you may increasingly be mine."

That was a letter that made me quiver, but a later one puzzled me. "Since our last meeting, minutes are years and miles whole continents, but I have learned that fierce emotion will pitch one from the heights to terrible abysses in spite of a careless forgetfulness, unless we see straight. Man's instinctive, often awkward, search for happiness is actually his reaching for God: the universal desire to unite with one's Creator. I love you and I am happy with you. And in you my search finds its answer. But, for the time being, we must content ourselves with our lighthearted meetings."

I put the letters back in the box and try to understand.

Summer's End, 1928

In the saddle, in the lake, talking around a campfire, getting to know a few people well, and being paid for doing all the things I like best—what a summer it has been! Out of the two months at Camp Kinni Kinnic, two events stand out—one touched me, the other touched me and Bill. Perhaps that is what ever happens: from a landscape blurring into memory there are summits seen in the mind, held in the heart.

On a warm July night we were alerted to the northern lights, and several of us went to the field that slopes down to the lake to watch the display. We lay on our backs in the evening-damp grass, and it was like being under a tent top as streamers of color shifted across the sky and were reflected in the lake. It lasted an hour or more, then dimmed and slowly faded away. When the colors diminished, the moon coming over the ridge to the east gave a steady glow to the night. Dixie, one of the counselors and a good friend, said she supposed I would write about what we had just seen.

"Indeed I will. Everything is grist to a writer's mill, but could I ever do justice to the aurora?"

"You can always try."

"Sometimes I think I could live on beauty."

"You can't, on beauty alone, if you expect to pay your bills."

What a comedown her words were after that hour of wonder!

The other event was the last time I saw Bill, at the end of August. It was the Sabbath, so I would not be teaching, and I was not needed at camp. The Brills gave me the whole day off. "Be back by dark" was my time limit. We had been planning the day for weeks in our letters, and when it finally came it was bright and warm. I felt that we had forever before us, and that's the way I always feel when I'm with Bill—as if we had all the time there was or would be, just as if our knowing each other had nothing to do with time. But after what happened today, I am not so sure.

We had a picnic luncheon, and on the large-scale map we had found a point where the Long Trail crossed the road, and it was there that Bill could leave his car. Up the trail we went, through woodland, up and up to a ridge. Seas of green forests rolled away from us on every side. The air was still, a few clouds traversed the sky. We passed a fire lookout, and there we left our picnic luncheon, the basket tucked away in a coign of rocks. The tower would be a good place to eat, and we would have to return that way in any case. Without the basket we were much freer. On and on we went, meeting occasional hikers and sharing information about the trail and the weather. We passed a spring, where we filled our canteen with delicious water. We talked, but not nearly so much as we generally did. It seemed good to be silent on that high ridge of the world.

A poem of Leonora Speyer's was in my mind, and, when we stopped for a moment to take the expanse of forest land and sky into us, I said it:

> Measure me, sky! Tell me I reach by a
> song
> Nearer the stars: I have been little so
> long.

63

Weigh me, high wind! What will your
  wild scales record?
Profit of pain, joy by the weight of a
  word.
Horizon, reach out! Catch at my
  hands, stretch me taut,
Rim of the world: widen my eyes by a
  thought.

How many miles we walked, how many heights
we gained, we did not know, only that we reached a
time when it seemed good to turn back and retrace
our steps. The sky had begun to haze and when we
finally reached the fire tower, mist was coming over
the distant ranges. We retrieved our picnic basket
and climbed up into the tower. It offered shelter, and
soon there was no view at all as the mist thickened
and rain came pattering down. Sitting on the bare
floor, backs against the metal wall, we satisfied our
hunger. We were dry and there was plenty of time
before the light changed and signified the end to our
day. We talked then, and our words were a continua-
tion of all we had been saying to each other for the
past year, but something new was added.

"How deep the arrow went," Bill said, and in my
mind I saw those two hearts carved into the bark of a
tree with an arrow piercing them, linking them.

We knew we were in love, and we could talk
about that with a delirious joy, but the next
thought—which might have been marriage—was as
remote as the mountains now lost in mist and rain.
Our friendship which had been growing and deepen-
ing every time we saw each other should have
fulfillment, but how was that to be? I had been afraid
to love, thinking it would upset my life, put me off

course; yet, what faced me now was the necessity to be true to love, as true as I was to myself in my insistence to lead my own life.

As for Bill, I knew he had "promises to keep" in the care of his elderly mother in Rochester, New York, whose support he was and whom he visited frequently. As the rain tapped on the metal roof of the fire tower, he told me he was wary of marriage. "Our friendship has been so perfect. You have not wanted to possess me or dominate me, just love me. Let us go on this way." There was a yearning in me that made me wonder if friendship could go on forever, if it must not in time become something else.

It was comforting to nestle in his arms, to say the only words I could say, had never said to anyone else and knew that I never would say to anyone but Bill. Love was my reason for being. I felt safe in Bill's embrace, and yet the future was so unsure. In our bare shelter on the mountaintop I felt in the presence of forces beyond ourselves.

Then he told me about his eyes, about a condition that might in time take his sight. "It would not be fair to you to put this upon you, if it happens."

I would not listen and with lips and words I hushed him. I could not believe that such a thing could happen to Bill, of all people, so I put what he was saying out of my mind. Later, much later, he said something that pierced me as the arrow had the two hearts we had seen on the tree.

"It will be better if we do not see each other for a while."

"But we can still write letters?"

"No, not even letters. We must go our separate ways—to see."

Yet, even as he spoke, his arms were around me. The world about us was all but lost in mist. It was as if we were on a last outpost of time; perhaps, for us, it was just that.

When the rain ceased, the light soon began to dim, and we knew we must leave our shelter. The downward trail back to the place on the road where the car had been left would be slippery and slow-going. We made it all right, and we got back to the camp gate before it was fully dark. When we said good-by, it was as if by mutual consent we added no endearments to the final word. Stumbling alone over the path to my cabin, I clung to the feel of his arms around me, the press of his lips on mine.

Once in the cabin, I moved around in the dark as quietly as I could, but there was little need—the seven children were sleeping soundly, and rain was thrumming gently on the roof. There was no sleep for me, I had so much to think about. How could two fears be resolved: mine of love, his of marriage? As often happens in exaltation or adversity, my thoughts shaped themselves into a poem, scribbled in the darkness to be rewritten in the morning.

October 15, 1928

Cleve came in tonight with a copy of my poem, which he had seen in the *Herald Tribune*. Nothing would do but that he should read it to me, and I listened, almost as if I had not written it.

AFTER PARTING
You did not know—what?
That your heart could be a world of
shattered stars

Whirling with a thousand broken bits
of memories,
And your throat so full of aching,
straining things
That your thoughts could be a travesty
of thinking,
Filtering over the bleak dust of your
barren mind;
And you would be lost when the light
faded
That led you on so long a way.
You were afraid when you heard your
soul cry
So terribly, so very terribly all night
long.
But oh, poor fumbler after tortuous
things,
What you did not know was that you
could love.

He didn't say anything for all of five minutes,
and what could I say that hadn't already been said?
Then his comment came, almost accusingly, "You're
in love, but not with me."

"No, not with you."

"This is what your work needs," and his tone
was authoritative. "You won't be talking about human emotions anymore, you'll be them. This is
without a doubt the best thing you have done."

"Coming from you, Cleve, that means something."

"May I take you out to dinner?"

Of course I said yes. Cleve has been so critical of
me, so superior with me; this time he was almost

respectful. Something in me basked. Do we all hunger for appreciation, or am I the only one who feels myself growing under it?

How glad I am to have Sinna! He is a real little dog now, sturdier than ever after his summer on the farm at Mountainville. I talk to him and, cocking his head this way and that, he seems to understand. I am trying to see straight about marriage. Perhaps it isn't all that important. To love, to care, to create in some way or another so that one is part of the creativity that is God, these are important. Yet to love another with heart and soul and mind is to make a commitment, and isn't this marriage?

November 10, 1928

The work on Bob's book is very nearly finished. He comes in two or three evenings a week and goes over the pages I've typed. Sometimes he makes changes and, when he does, that means a whole page has to be retyped, and still he comes up with one more experience that he feels should be in the story.

"Must you have all those ghastly descriptions of fighting? I know you are a skilled boxer, but I didn't think you were such a fighter."

"Oh, sure, that's life in the raw, you have to tell it the way it is."

"If you bring me many more additions, I'll never get it typed by Christmas."

"What's the hurry?"

"I want to get it on to a publisher's desk first thing in the New Year. That seems an auspicious time."

We discussed titles—"In the Wheatfields," "My

Summer Adventure," several others, but none seemed exactly right, so Bob suggested that I list them all on the first page and we let the publisher choose. That made sense. He says my name should be on it, but I say no, that it is his story, but that he can dedicate it to me. When he leaves, I feel lonelier than ever. It's curious, but on the trail that day, when I said Leonora Speyer's poem to Bill, I didn't say the last verse. Perhaps I couldn't remember it, perhaps it didn't seem to fit with the day. I say it often now.

> Sky, be my depth; wind, be my width
>   and my height;
> World, my heart's span: loneliness
>   wings for my flight!

I try not to think about Bill, not to hunger for the sound of his voice on the phone or for the sight of his handwriting on a letter, but it's hard. He had said "for a while." How long is a while? I wonder that as I do the articles for the *American*, work on Bob's book, and ease my heart with poems.

December 20, 1928

Just as I was packing to go home for Christmas the phone rang. "Long distance calling—" It was Bill, calling from Boston. We must have talked a long time, but I can remember only three of his words, "I love you." And I repeated them.

From some dim recess of memory comes a lovely line, "Set me as a seal upon thine heart."

1929
January to August

1929
JANUARY TO AUGUST

January 20, 1929

Today I had luncheon with an editor!

It seemed a good idea to put Bob's story with The Macmillan Company. They are right here in New York, and it could be delivered by hand. I had heard that Miss Louise Seaman was a fine editor and that books done by her were successful. At the Public Library, when doing my assignments, I read several adventure stories, and those published by Macmillan seemed to stand out above the others. So I left the big package—typed pages and several titles, all neatly wrapped the way we had learned to do at the Franklin School when I never knew how useful it would be, and a note to Miss Seaman. I requested her to get in touch with me, as I could be reached more easily than my brother.

I never expected a phone call, but only a few days later, it came. She asked me to come to her office and said she would like to take me out to luncheon. I wanted to ask her if she liked the book, but I held myself in check. Obviously she did or she wouldn't want to talk with me about it.

She's just like her voice—warm and friendly, and young; she's very good-looking, too. I didn't feel shy with her, just natural. She took me to the Brevoort, almost across the street from her office, and when the waiter came with the menu, she asked me what I would like. Frogs' legs sounded interesting and unusual, so that is what we both had.

She talked and I listened, except when she urged me to tell her more about my brother. That was easy, for I've loved Bob as long as I've known him. She said that his adventure was one of the best stories that had come to her desk in a long time and that she had not had to read it all before she knew she wanted to publish it.

"When I Was a Harvester," she said, and so gave the book its title. We talked about pictures, a map, the jacket, and all sorts of details, but I was so eager to get to a telephone to give Bob the news that I couldn't take in all that she was saying; besides, I found that a certain amount of attention has to be given to frogs' legs if you expect to get anything from them.

Bob came over after work and I told him everything.

"If it's that easy to get a book published, maybe I shouldn't be trying to learn the hotel business."

"It has to be written first."

"That's right."

"And before it's written it has to be experienced."

"Right again."

"And you can't disappoint Father."

74

Bob smiled, the smile I had learned to know so well when we were working on his pages, the smile of sweet agreement.

I told him all that would happen before it became a book and that it would take time. Miss Seaman had said that it would be read by other editors, then it would be copy-edited; after that it would go into galleys, which would be returned to us for checking. It was then that changes could be made if they were necessary, but I warned Bob that we must try not to make any changes, as they would cost us money. She felt the book needed pictures and suggested that many could be found in newspaper files. "She expects that you can supply a good photograph of yourself and Ronno. I asked if my friend, Eunice Stephenson, could submit a design for the jacket, and Miss Seaman said yes, that they are always on the lookout for good artists. Then we got to the contract. She would like to discuss terms with you, Bob."

"Terms! That sounds like a business."

"But of course, a book is a business venture."

"You should be the one to talk terms."

"No, Bob, it's your book."

"You did a lot of work on it."

"You gave me the material to work with."

"It doesn't seem quite right."

"It's right, all right. Don't you remember, when you gave me those forty pages I gave you fifty dollars? You didn't want to take it, but I insisted. It was a business arrangement from the start, not signed and sealed, but just as real."

And then he smiled again.

February 2, 1929

I've just finished an interview for the *American*, my first face-to-face with a person, Edith Keating, an aerial photographer. She found her niche in life and it is in the air, but her work is proportioned between earth and sky, because, when she isn't flying, she is a departmental executive. I asked her where she preferred to be and she said, "In the air. I feel safer up there." She gave me her picture and autographed it for me.

February 4, 1929

And now it looks as if my life will be proportioned between wheels and people, because Father is going on a business trip to the West Coast and has asked me to go with him. I telephoned Bill at his office in Boston to say good-by. We agreed not to write during the month I would be away, but to see each other just as soon as I returned. If love is strong as death, as the Bible says, it must be as strong as distance.

My journal can hold only swift impressions of all that I'll be seeing, and probably none of the conversations I'll be having, but I'll write as much as I can so it will be within these pages when I want to return to it. There will be time for reading when Father is busy or when he gets behind his paper, and I'll have plenty of time to think. The rolling rhythm of train wheels day after day, the distances drawing my eyes will be conducive to long thoughts; and mountains, higher than any I have ever seen before, will stimulate me.

Since Bill's telephone call before Christmas I want time to think about us and the possibility that is ahead. Sometime. What a word! What does it mean?

I can remember, when I was little, saying to people, "I love you two bushels"—or ten, or twenty, or however greatly I was inspired, for love then was something that could be measured and dealt out in separate amounts to different persons. Now I am beginning to see that there is no measure to love, no unit of measure, no one or a thousand, for it is all the same. It flows to all alike. It is all around us. It is what keeps us in the heart of God.

This love of mine is not happiness, but it is strong, terribly strong, and yet insecure. So long as I love Bill everything of me is his. I cannot hold more than one star in my hands. Of myself I am sure, but of him I am not sure; yet why do I want to be sure? Where do these thoughts come from? Perhaps from my need to understand. I have just begun to glimpse what love is, and that it is what life is all about.

February 9, 1929

It was overnight to Chicago, then we changed trains and settled in—parlor chairs by day, sleepers at night, and the diner, where we enjoyed everything, especially things that were new and we'd never tasted before. Father is good to travel with; he knows how to leave you alone, because he wants to be left alone to follow his pursuits, mostly the stock reports on those interminable pages of *The Wall Street Journal*. It was cold and gray when we left Chicago and the same as we got farther west, especially through Kansas, where every mile seemed like every other mile. When we came over the Divide and into northern New Mexico in the early morning, I was dazzled, not only by the mountains but by the mesas of glittering snow in the bright sunlight. When we dropped into desert country it was fully as beautiful, but in another way—expansive.

I spend lots of time on the observation platform, and it's easy to get into conversation with other people. Most of them don't want so much to talk as to have me listen to them, but it is all interesting, and I make jottings in my notebook of unusual expressions, situations, names. It may be useful. If I tuck all this away, I'll know where to find it when I need it.

We reached Phoenix late at night and went to our hotel. Oh, to revel in a hot bath after all those days in the train! I finished *The World's Illusion*. It was wonderful to see, within the tight span of a book, how all mankind is really working out of materiality into spirituality.

We are to spend a whole week in Phoenix, and I'll be on my own much of the time. There is glowing sunshine, cool breezes, dawns that skyrocket over distant mountains, and sunsets of splintered gold. A white half moon looks like a lamb on its back, kicking playfully at the stars. Solitary, sentinel cacti in the desert look grotesque and often whimsical. Some of the queer rock formations look like part of a world before time began, and then there is the rich greenness where irrigation has been introduced. I've never seen, or tasted, such fruits and vegetables.

Today we drove with a friend of Father's to Castle Hot Springs, and I swam in a pool where the water was a hundred and twenty degrees, then in another pool it was cooler, and in a third pool the way water generally is. We went to a rodeo at a little frontier town, Wickenburg, then over the Apache Trail to Roosevelt Dam. Painted cliffs! Walls of Bronze! Ends of the Earth! Then we followed the Superior Highway through narrow canyons of glowering red rocks, like a Valhalla of forgotten gods. On our way to Sentinel we saw many mirages across the desert, and my heart ached for the pioneers who had followed mirages in their terrible need for water. Some towns along the way are nothing but names now, and there are rivers with no water in them. We stopped at Yuma, where it never rains, went past miles of sand dunes, and suddenly we were in the voluptuous fertility of the Imperial Valley of California.

February 23, 1929

We left El Centro through the Carriso Gorge to San Diego, and at Coronado Beach we had a real swim. It's a perfect beach, and the sand has gold leaf in it. The salt smell of the sea was invigorating after the arid breath of the desert, and the water of the Pacific was so cold that we had to swim hard to get warm. San Diego is charming, so many little houses with neat gardens, trees, and a lush tidiness evident. We crossed the border into Mexico and visited the racetrack at Tijuana, a beautiful place, set in a surround of low hills. Father gave me twenty dollars to bet with, and I lost all but two, then I stopped. He had better luck, or perhaps he knows more about horses. I chose them from their names, which they didn't live up to.

Los Angeles seemed a noisy, confused city.

Pasadena was beautiful. We saw the Mission Play, and I was stirred, as I always am, by anything having to do with deep truths. Hollywood seemed elegant but vulgar, then there was Mt. Lowe, an ostrich farm, a lion farm, and the train to San Francisco. Much of the route was along the shore—white breakers, sand dunes, great cliffs, fantastic trees on one side, and on the other golden poppies, blue lupin, green fields, and rich vegetation. I gazed far across the ocean in the early evening and it looked truly pacific; the sky was like a scroll of heaven with the first stars telling their stories. San Francisco is hilly and fascinating— the Golden Gate Bridge, the Aquarium, Gumps, Chinatown, the Sky Line Drive, and food such as I had never dreamed of before.

This part of the trip is over; still to be enjoyed are the three days on the train homeward bound. We have had such fun, and I think Father and I know each other better than we ever have before. But when he introduces me to his friends he says, "My daughter"; he never adds, "She's a writer." Will I go on all my life hungering for just that measure of appreciation for what I am as a person in myself?

There's been a story moving in my mind, so I spent much of the time on the train writing it—the impact made on a young girl from the East when she meets the West, and the West to her is a handsome cowboy who can ride bronchos and rope steers. It was the rodeo at Wickenburg that gave me the setting and a rather pallid young woman on the train from Chicago who gave me the other character. Most of the story is what I've done in my imagination, but at least the setting is as true as I can make it.

March 8, 1929

Arrived back in Buffalo in a raging blizzard.

March 10, 1929

Bill met my train at Grand Central Station and we went to Childs' for breakfast. All the news I had for him paled at his news: he is leaving for England in three weeks for a position in his company's office in London. It is a promotion in many ways—salary, responsibility, opportunity; but what does it mean for us?

April 9, 1929

This is the night I shall remember all my life—it is the climax of the past weeks, it wraps up all Bill and I have been saying for the past two years. We went to the theater and saw *Holiday,* then we went to the St. Regis for a late supper and danced. After that we walked up to Central Park and snuggled into one of the horse-drawn carriages. Bill told the driver to go very slowly; we wanted the evening never to end. It was dark and quiet in the Park. Distant lights in tall buildings dimmed, only streetlights glimmered; except for faraway traffic, the only sounds were the clopping of hooves. It was edging toward dawn when Bill left me at 243.

The *Queen Mary* sails at noon, but he does not want me to come down to the dock, nor do I want to. It was better to say good-by here. Is every ending a beginning? We do not know when we will meet again, but we could not feel the way we do about each other if it were not going to be all right sometime. For the time being we have ruled out any thought of marriage. Months ago I had resolved my fear of love, but I sense in our silences that Bill has not yet entirely resolved his fear of marriage. I wanted to write him a bon voyage letter, but knew that if I said anything at all I would say too much, so I made up a riddle, printed it, and sealed it in an envelope for him to open after the ship had sailed.

> We stood on a river's edge
> And saw infinity before us;
> We stood on a mountaintop
> And felt infinity tower o'er us;
> We looked in each other's eyes
> And—
> What was it there we saw
> That made us press close,
> Clinging together?

I keep Bill in the quietness of my mind and talk with him as if we were in the garden at John's or standing on Timp. And there is always Sinna to talk aloud to. He's a wise little fellow and by his presence he helps to fill some of the emptiness I feel. Bill asked me to write him, but he said that except for an occasional letter he would keep in touch with me by cable. It will take him time, and more than time, to establish himself in a new country, with a different approach to his work. I am back at my familiar pattern of work, research for the *American*, assembling pictures for Bob's book, putting into shape the story I wrote on the train. More than ever, I feel an increasing capacity to get on with things.

April 11, 1929

While at the *Herald Tribune*, going through files of pictures, I went past the office of Mrs. Irita Van Doren, who is in charge of book reviewing. That gave me an idea, so I made a telephone call and requested an appointment to see her. When we sat facing each other, I asked her if I might review books for her. She didn't say, "What qualifications have you?" to which I would have had to reply, "None." Instead we went on talking about books, and travel, and dogs, and poetry, all kinds of things, the way people talk when they are comfortable with each other. She is a small, gentle person with the charm of the South in her voice and manner. Half an hour later I left with three of the new spring novels and a promise that she would have more for me when I brought in my reviews in a week's time. "Keep to about two hundred and fifty words," she said, and that was all the direction I had. I like people who give a free rein. Horses always respond better when reins are held lightly.

A cable has just come from the ship. Two words, the answer to my riddle—"Each other." But there were other words that were invisible. So often, perhaps almost always, Bill ended a meeting with "And the rest you know." Those words, and what they meant to me, were in the cable, but only my eyes could see them.

April 25, 1929

Carl, that old darling of my childhood days, telephoned and asked me out for dinner and the evening. He is a senior at Princeton and has just completed his thesis on the Monroe Doctrine. We had a wonderful time—dinner, then the theater, and after that dancing. He has grown to such a fine and handsome man and was happy to talk about God. After graduation next month he and his sister are going to France.

And where will I be next month? With Eunice, my artist friend, at Turn of River near Stamford, Connecticut. How one thing leads to another! Mrs. Howard at the Frankl Gallery introduced me to Mildred on *The American Magazine*, who introduced me to Eunice one day when she brought work in to the *American*. She is a commercial artist, and I liked her from the start. Eunice is one of the few people to whom I have talked about Bill. She knows the emptiness in my life right now, but I think she does not know the uncertainty, and she has asked me to spend the summer with her. It will be as wonderful for Sinna as for me to be out of the city and in the country.

April 28, 1929

[Cable from London]

HEIGHO DARLING MOVING MODEST HOTEL ENSURING MORE SOLITUDE BUSY HAPPY THANKS CABLE LETTER THRILLED SO MUCH LOVE

May 5, 1929

In a matter of days it all became possible. I was able to sublet the apartment until the lease is up in September, and my work can be done anywhere. So now I am part of Eunice's family, which includes her ten-year-old son, Gregg, and her housekeeper, Mrs. Brown. The springtime world is tiptoe with wonder. The Rippowam River, really just an oversized brook, runs through woodland, races through fields, and almost loses itself in marshy places where cowslips grow in clumps of golden color. Buds on the trees are ready to burst into blossom and leaf after a succession of warm days. Birds carol exultantly. There is a feeling of discovery everywhere as growing moves to fruition. I am on the edge of discovery, too. There is so much ahead for Bill and me. It doesn't seem to matter that we have to wait a little while longer. I'm reading Emerson and keep finding thoughts of his that speak for me, like this: "to keep in the midst of the crowd with perfect sweetness the independence of solitude."

May 12, 1929

[Cable from London]

> BUSY DAYS SO MUCH TO DO BUT GETTING ORGANIZED PERSONALLY AND ANTICIPATING MORE PLAY FINE HAPPY GRATEFUL ALL LOVE

Eunice has had a portion of the field dug up for a vegetable garden. I made a plan for it the way I used to do at Hillhurst. With Gregg's help I got it all

85

planted. Now, after a morning at my desk, or reading, I go out in the afternoon and work in the garden.
What a balanced and beautiful life this is.

May 19, 1929

[Cable from London]

AWFULLY HAPPY THRILLS CONTINUE ALL LOVE
THANKS FOR EVERYTHING

May 26, 1929

Our seeds, planted just ten days ago, are showing. I had a telegram from Loyola: "*Romance Magazine*
taking *Golden Ocean* at two cents a word. Check next
week. Congratulations." Three cheers, and that
means the check will be for a hundred and ten
dollars. The setting for that story was the wheatfields
of Saskatchewan, and I never would have been able
to picture it if Bob hadn't made it so vivid and my
research had not confirmed it. All the time I was
writing it I felt as if I were living in those fields of
waving grain.

June 10, 1929

Today we ate the firstfruits of the garden—
radishes!

June 11, 1929

[Cable from London]

BRAVO STORY RADISHES LETTERS WONDERFUL

GLORIOUS WEATHER COUNTRYSIDE BEAUTIFUL
DEEPEST LOVE

My life has resolved itself into great simplicities. I feel as if one hand was held out to Thoreau, who said, "Simplify, simplify," and the other hand to Katherine Mansfield, who said, "Oh, to be simple, as one would be before God." After a morning with words, an afternoon with weeds is in order, then a swim in the pool made by the Rippowam.

June 17, 1929

[Cable from Dublin]

CAN YOU IMAGINE YOU KNOW I REALLY BE-
LIEVE I SAW FAIRIES LAST NIGHT ALL LOVE

A letter came today, marked By Fast Ship. I held it in my hands, realizing that less than a week ago his hands had held it. It was a long letter, so I took it down to sit by the pool and read it alone and quietly, with only Sinna beside me. I'll share some of it with the family at supper tonight, but just for now it is for me.

"The first night, as I walked down Piccadilly, everything seemed familiar to me. I felt as if I had come home." Reading those words brought to me the feeling I had had when I was eighteen and went to England with Mother and Father and Bobby. He went on, drawing pictures with words: "During the peak of early-morning traffic, there was a flock of sheep being skillfully guided across the teeming Strand by an alert dog and a sleepy lad. . . . Men and women around Covent Garden Market before breakfast carry the most amazing loads on their heads. One chap had eleven hampers about the size of ladies' hatboxes, piled to the sky, it seemed. And there were short fat women sitting beside huge crates of fruit. . . . Near Marble Arch there was an old, old lady, with stringy white hair and but a few teeth, standing in the gutter playing on a harp with even fewer strings. It was raining, but she had a twinkle and a smile. . . . Standing on the railway platform at Reading, I heard a screech and a flash, and the Plymouth boat train passed. . . . Some of the old, very old, pubs have such odd names: Ye Old Dive Hotel, The Running Footman, Carryme Inn. . . . I stood by the Sanctuary Stone in Liverpool. It was the bad debtor's retreat, for a man could not be arrested even by law as long as he was on that stone. . . . Railway posters are works of art, showing the beauty spots of England and Scotland. . . . As I walked home from the office to my flat in Bruton Street, thinking of you and hoping there might be a letter from you, my heart leaped because there was one."

June 26, 1929

We are knee-deep in June. Lilacs have given way to rambler roses. Daisies and buttercups brighten the fields. The garden thrives. This morning, when I woke up, a scarlet tanager was swinging and singing on a branch just outside my window. It was a moment of flame and perhaps it was a harbinger, for there was a letter in the mail from Loyola. She has sold *Her Real Debut* to something called *Complete Love Novel Magazine*. That's the story I wrote about the girl who fell in love with the West—the bored young debutante who thought love was a mockery, but out of the dust of the rodeo a new life was born.

[Cable from London]

HEIGHO DEAREST EVERYTHING FINE VERY BUSY
ALL LOVE

My bank account is growing and that's good. Whatever is ahead for me, it will help to have funds.

July 13, 1929

[Cable from London]

WELL AND HAPPY ALL LOVE DEAREST

A message from England should be largesse for one day, but there was more—a copy of the magazine with *Golden Ocean*. There were no plans that could not easily be changed, so I put a call through to Bob to ask him to have dinner with me to celebrate. Eunice gave me her first rough sketch of the jacket for *When I Was a Harvester*, and I knew Bob would like to see it. "Tell him to make any changes now," Eunice said, "for I can do them easily." Bob liked the jacket design and said it was correct, even to the white tip on Ronno's tail, but he took a dim view of *Romance Magazine*, not of my story. He liked it. "But I think you shouldn't show it to Mother and Father."

"But why, Bob? It means I'm getting somewhere."

"It's sort of lurid."

"You have to start somewhere, Bob, and I'm glad that Loyola is finding magazines willing to pay me two cents for every word."

July 17, 1929

[Cable from London]

GOING LE TOUQUET WEEKEND ALL LOVE
DEAREST

August 1, 1929

What a long time without a cable! I tell Eunice
that Bill must be away, or very busy. Perhaps there
will be a letter tomorrow that will make up for the
weeks between.

1929
September to November

1929
SEPTEMBER TO NOVEMBER

September, 1929

Weeks have become a month and summer has passed. I have watched the flowers in the fields change in color and character. The garden has been a continuing harvest, giving us more every day. Now the first leaves fall and winds toss them over the yellowing grass. In the last warmth of a fading season, the air has the scent of drying things. And still, my heart has no answer. Why is there no word in all these weeks? I continue writing letters, but resist cabling. I do not want to bother him if he is very busy.

Three nights of rain, three misty days, and now leaves are falling everywhere. I cannot stand it, so tomorrow I shall go in to Stamford and send a cable.

September 9, 1929

[Cable from Stamford]

WHERE HAS THE GENTLEMAN FROM PERU GONE?

September 10, 1929

[Cable from London]

> WROTE YOU LAST WEDNESDAY A MOST DIFFI-
> CULT LETTER. HAPPINESS IN A NEW INTEREST
> HERE HAS SUDDENLY TURNED TO UTTER CON-
> FUSION AND DOUBT. AM PRAYING FOR LIGHT
> AND SEEK YOUR UNSELFED UNDERSTANDING.

September 11, 1929

[Cable from Liverpool]

> AWAY TILL FRIDAY FOG LIFTING PLEASE STAND
> FAST DEAR

September 11, 1929

[Cable from Stamford]

> WHATEVER HAPPENS I KNOW THAT GOD IS
> GUIDING YOU

So, there is a letter on the way, but the second cable makes me feel that when it comes, it may be out of date.

September 14, 1929

The letter is in my hands. I might as well have a stone. I took it down to the pool, the place where the river makes its turn, and held it in my hands, letting my eye travel over that familiar writing—my name,
94

the address, the British stamp. It was a long time before I opened it. Sinna nudged me, then put his head on my knee almost as if he thought I needed him near.

". . . I am deeply in love with a girl I met in Le Touquet. Her name is Rebecca, she is an American, and she has been touring Europe with her mother. We have been seeing a lot of each other since that weekend, and tremendous things have been happening to me. To my amazement, I am finding that all fear of every kind has completely vanished and I am eager and ready for marriage. It is something I have never known before and everything within me tells me it is right. . . . In your last two letters, more beautiful than ever, you remind me of my right to freedom and happiness, and that your dearest prayer is for my good, if not with you then away from you. And, behold, it has happened in this most extraordinary way! . . . I know of your love for me. Your confidence and encouragement have been support and inspiration through many a trying hour. And now—yes, the heart has a way of its own. Nothing can ever erase my memories of our times together— on Timp, over winding roads, by open fires, in wind and rain. But now I pray with all my heart that you will be glad for me in my newfound happiness."

Could this be true? I asked myself. The date of the letter was September 4, and the cable of the 10th said something quite different, as did the one of the 11th.

I went back to the house. Eunice met me at the door. "Is everything all right?" she asked.

"Yes, with Bill," I said, and presumably that was

true. Anything I might say otherwise would be betraying him, and that I would not do. I told her I was walking in to Stamford to send a cable, that I might be late and not to wait supper.

Her eyes were moist and warm, her cheeks flushed as they often are after hours of work at her drawing board. I wanted to put my arms around her, to feel hers around me, but I knew that if I did, I would dissolve into weeping. She sensed some strain in me and let me go my way. It was a hard cable to send and yet, in all honor, I felt obliged to send it.

[Cable from Stamford]

LETTER RECEIVED HAPPY IN YOUR HAPPINESS
PLEASE UNDERSTAND CONTINUANCE OF
FRIENDSHIP IS IMPOSSIBLE

Midnight

There are roads the heart must go over
Before it can learn to forget a lover;
Until sinews know their release
And the nerves find subtle peace
In loss that frees by creating
Voids the soul has had in waiting.

The leisured heart shall learn to find
Sustenance of its own kind,
Knowing sometime, some tomorrow
Will lift the lethargy of sorrow.

September 16, 1929

Back to my work, back to the garden, back to walks in the woods with my wondering little Sinna, back to living one day after the other, hoping the futility that beset me during the first years in New York would not sweep over me again. Thoughtful Eunice asked no questions; Mrs. Brown made all my favorite foods as if she felt I needed to be kept eating, and Gregg seemed always ready to do whatever chore he could for me. No one asked me what had happened, and for that I ever bless them. How could I say? What did I know?

A bulky package has come from Macmillan, the galley proofs of *When I Was a Harvester*. I'll check them as well as I can, then take them in to New York for Bob to go over and return to Miss Seaman.

September 21, 1929

[Cable from London]

> THIS EXPERIENCE HAS BEEN PRICELESS IN RE-
> MOVING ALL FEAR AND THEN PROVING BEYOND
> QUESTION THAT YOU ARE THE ONLY ONE
> PLEASE HOW SOON CAN YOU COME?

September 22, 1929

[Cable from Stamford]

> SOON

Tonight I told them at supper that I would be leaving for England in about a month, or as soon as everything could be arranged, to marry Bill. And glad was I that whatever might have been said before had been locked in my heart. How happy they looked and were in their different ways—Eunice, Mrs. Brown, Gregg. They are very dear to me.

The next mail brought a long letter from Bill—so easy to read, so exciting, and as light as a feather in my hands. And within the words I could hear the mellow tone of his voice. "My experience seems like a queer dream. No harm has been done to the other party in any way because of it, so I can only be grateful for the strange working of events which showed me where my affection truly lies. I'll tell you all about it later. There is so much to talk about now." And there is! He said he had written my father asking for my hand "if she will give it." He went on for pages with all kinds of details, and in every few words was a word of endearment.

". . . there are a million things to talk about but I can't think of anything but you, so I'll turn in and lie wide-eyed for hours planning weekends and trips and seeing Scottish mountains and Irish lakes, Yorkshire moors and the Cornish coast, and glorious evenings at home reading in front of a coal fire and talking. Oh, my darling, you are mine and I am forever your Bill."

A writer is generally a curious person, but this time I did not care to know what had happened at Le Touquet and in the weeks following. A designing girl, aided by an equally designing mother, had set her cap for a charming, unattached man. It sounded like a story for *Romance Magazine*, but this was one story that I would not write. The unknown Rebecca had unwittingly done me a good turn, and for this I was grateful. Bill knew now that marriage was something to be faced, that it could not always be avoided in a relationship that went beyond friendship.

September 24, 1929

[Cable from Liverpool]

ECSTATIC COME EARLIEST CONVENIENT SIX
MONTHS QUARANTINE FOREIGN DOGS WRITTEN
YOUR FAMILY SURELY LOVE'S FULFILLMENT

I had intended to go into New York within the
next few days to see Miss Seaman and deliver Eunice's finished jacket, but after that cable, "soon"
could not be soon enough. I took the noon train into
the city and got back late. Eunice was waiting for me.
We sat at the kitchen table and had a snack, but more
important than food was the news I had for her.
Proof of how much Miss Seaman liked the jacket was
the nice fat check that she would be receiving in a few
days, as well as the possibility of more work for
Macmillan. Eunice has a motherly way, so she soon
hustled me off to bed, saying she knew I was tired
after my long day and we could talk tomorrow. I'm
not a bit tired, and I want to write everything down,
because it has been one of the most impressive days
of my life.

On the train going in I made a list of all the things
there were to do. If I do that, then check them off one
by one, the number doesn't seem so intimidating.
First I delivered the picture to Miss Seaman, and she
told me the astounding news that the book had been
accepted as a selection of the Junior Literary Guild.
My news was equally astounding to her, so we made
a luncheon date for next week. I went to the American Consul to be sure my passport was in order, to

the American Express to see when a sailing would be possible, and then to the owner of the apartment to wind up the lease at 243 and make arrangements with a mover to put my things in storage until I could send for them from London. I phoned the *Herald Tribune* and asked to see Mrs. Van Doren next week. Last thing I did was to send a cable to Bill.

Bob took me out to dinner. It was comforting to sit across a table from him and look into his warm brown eyes. To him, as to no one else, I poured out the whole sequence of the past few weeks and what the next few weeks held. He was amazed and delighted, but when I told him the stupendous news about his book, he leaned across the table and kissed me.

"Think of what that means, Bob. You'll have ready-made readers up and down and across the country."

"Will it mean more money?"

"Yes, quite a lot. Miss Seaman said there would be an advance of a thousand dollars."

"Then that is yours."

"Oh, Bobby—"

"You'll need it in a new country, a new life. You may need it to come home if you don't like it over there."

"Oh, Bobby—"

"When are you going?"

"I sent Bill a cable today that I would be sailing on the *Bremen*, October 25."

"What will happen to Sinna?"

"He's going with me. Bill thought of that even before I did."

"Do Mother and Father know?"

"Not yet from me, but Bill has written to them. I'm going up to Hillhurst the end of next week."

And now, having put down for myself the events of this one day, I must write Bill the letter I promised him.

October 5, 1929

I've been at the farm for a week and it is as always, as if I'd never been away. The pattern of life moves in its orderly fashion—Father goes in to his office in Buffalo every morning, and Mother talks with Maria about the household. Plans are made for the day, and its events may include me and they may not. I can always find Al in the barn, or Jim in the garden, or Andy polishing the Packard. Jinny is often here with her two boys, one a real toddler, the other a small babe. I look at her and think how is it that some people can do everything right—marry a lawyer with a growing practice, produce two fine boys? I watch her with the children, not enviously or with emulation but with the strangest feeling that this will not be for me. I don't know why. It's just that sometimes in life one knows without being told.

So I fit into the pattern more as the young sister home for a few days than the woman with life beckoning ahead, and I remind myself that Emerson said life is a struggle for freedom and the individual must assert himself through moral and intellectual integrity. To Miss Hyde I have always been a person, even when I was little. She has paid me a great compliment. She said, "I shall always think of you as being happy, for that is how I have always thought of you."

One day I went to Rochester to meet Bill's mother. She is very frail and quite old, and in her past there has been much sorrow and illness. She talked about Bill and told me stories of him when he was growing up, of his high standing in school and how, after college, he had planned to go on to law school; then his father died suddenly. Bill was just eighteen, and there was an older sister, who was an invalid, and a much younger brother and sister. There was only one thing for Bill to do—give up his own plans and take over his father's business for the sake of the family. So much she told me that I had not known, and it made me love him more. Over and over she said, "I think you can make him happy and that is what I pray for him. He has done so much for others all through the years. Now he needs a homelife of his own."

She gave me her engagement ring, given to her more than fifty years ago. It's lovely, a small ruby in a crown-like setting of tiny seed pearls, and it fits me as it must have fit her when Lawrence first slipped it on her finger. It seems so right, now, to have an engagement ring.

October 8, 1929

When I came back from a ride with Bluemouse today, Andy and Maria were sitting at the kitchen table having their tea. I joined them because I wanted to talk with them about "the old country." They had left England when they were a young married couple and come to the United States, now I was going to England to be married. There was so much that I could learn from them. After I had finished my cup of tea, there were quite a few leaves in it, so I swirled them around and handed the cup to Andy to read my fortune. He studied the leaves for a long time, every now and then taking the tip of his penknife to look under a leaf.

"What do you see, Andy?"

"There's a fine man in your cup, taller than you, with dark-brown hair and a spring to his way of walking. See that little leaf? That's him. And there's happiness for the two of you, that's at the rim right down to the bottom. See that small thin leaf? That's your pencil. It's not near the top, but there's nothing between it and the top. That means success."

"When, Andy?"

"Not soon, but sure."

Again he lifted a leaf to look under it.

"What are you trying to find?"

"Something I can't see. It's like a shadow. I don't rightly know where it is or what it means, but it isn't going to interfere with your happiness."

"Andy, you told me what color hair the man in my life—in my cup—has. What color are his eyes?"

Andy studied the leaves that were beginning to dry and shift their positions. He shook his head. "I can't seem to see his eyes."

"They're gray, Andy, and beautiful." Then I asked Andy if he had any advice for me and my life with Bill.

"Just remember that there may come a time when you'll feel contrary, and there may come a time when he'll feel contrary, but don't you both feel contrary at the same time."

103

I've been going through the things stored away in the R.I.P. box, and I'm destroying a great deal, just keeping a few reminders as waymarks, and the Diaries that cover eleven years of my life. What a trial I must have been to my elders! Such determination for independence! Such fury at convention! Some of the early poems do have a lyrical quality, but I was so extravagant with words. Luxury as a way of life drew my scorn, but I luxuriated in words. And love, what did I know about it then to write about it as I did? My descriptions of nature were really good, and I was always on safe ground when writing about the weather. The poems did serve a purpose: my feelings got out in words on paper; they didn't rankle inside me.

Two cables have punctuated my days. They were telephoned, and I was lucky in being the one to answer the phone both times. I don't dare imagine what some people would have thought at a string of unsigned words whose meaning was only for me.

October 10, 1929

[Cable from London]

HAPPY BUSY THRILLED EAGER LOVE

October 15, 1929

[Cable from London]

GLORIOUS NEWS ROCHESTER SO HAPPY THANKS
DEEPEST LOVE

October 16, 1929

Today his letter written on the 9th came—five pages of that beloved handwriting that sings as it flows over the page. ". . . This afternoon your tiny but precious note written from New York in the midst of packing came . . . and the poem, 'O Darling Room,' is lovely. No doubt it speaks a bit for you in leaving East 36th Street. . . . Today I walked home from the office through back streets, thinking sweet thoughts of you and me, not unlike our 'pretending' thoughts of many a time together—of woodsmoke and cool pools and hills and sky and sheep. Can you know how my heart is actually leaping with eagerness these yearlong days? . . . Last evening, after an important meeting, I spent some time with Mr. Mangum. I had just returned from Manchester, where I secured the largest order our company here has yet had. He was in a genial mood and warned me of all the things he is going to tell you about me, especially how I gained the name of Pink Tea Willie. And then he said he was going to give me an interest in the company as a wedding present and put it in your name, by gosh! He has been so fine to me and really thinks I'm great.

"I know how awfully busy you are these last few weeks, dear, and will understand if you don't write—just a cable now and then, please. Soon, soon, you and Sinna will be sailing to me. They tell me I have only to cable the number of Sinna's permit to you. The actual permit should be given here to Van Oppen and Co., the carrying agents, who will meet the

Bremen, provide a suitable kennel, take care of clearance, etc., and take him to The Dog's Home, Hackbridge, Surrey. That is just a thirty-minute ride from London, where he will be excellently cared for and can be visited any day. . . . Darling, just two weeks from tomorrow—Southampton! Oh, dear God, I am so grateful."

I had need of the letter, for after dinner Father said he would like to have a talk with me. Everyone mysteriously disappeared and we were alone in the living room by the fire. I knew he had heard from Bill more than a week ago; I also knew that he would choose his own time to talk with me. He held the letter in his hand. How well I knew that writing, so legible, so well spaced.

Slowly, carefully, Father read the letter aloud. In it Bill told him, from a man's point of view, all that a man would want to know about his job, his salary, his prospects, his flat in London, the insurance policies he carried, his financial responsibility to his mother, the stocks he held. He even mentioned a Wassermann test, which meant nothing to me, but satisfied Father. Of course, Bill said he loved me.

After the reading was finished, neither of us said anything. It was Father's move. I had long known what I would do, and what Bill had done in words was, after all, only a formality.

"I want you to understand that neither your mother nor I have any objection. We wish you would wait until the spring, when we could be with you."

"To wait would waste time. Bill and I know what we want, and once we are married, we can get on with the business of living."

"You always seem to know what is right for you."

"I know that I love Bill. I have since I met him almost three years ago."

"And you are leaving soon for England?"

"In two weeks."

"Your mother and I will come over in the spring to visit you and to meet Bill."

That was the end of our conversation. When I said good night, he kissed me. The feel of his mustache was not so bristly as when I was a little girl.

Mother was waiting for me upstairs. All her love was in her eyes, in the embrace she folded me in, in her words about wanting me to be happy. She wished that I could have found someone nearer home, that I would not be so far away, but all I could say was that I must marry the one I love. We talked on for a while, but when we said good night I had the feeling that I had from father, that they understood, as they had four years ago about my being a writer.

And now as I face myself in my own room for the last time—for tomorrow night I'll be on the train to New York—I think of Cleve and Ben and others I have had good times with. It is Bill who loves me not just for what I am now, a person, but for what I may be someday, a writer. This was the key he turned that let him into my life.

October 19, 1929

Now I am back at Turn of River

[Cable from London]

YOUR LETTER SO WONDERFUL OH AM SO HAPPY
AND CONFIDENT MY DEAREST SINNA PERMIT
NUMBER EYE DEE NINETY ONE THIRTY EIGHT
MAILING UNNECESSARY SO MUCH LOVE

October 23, 1929

[Cable from London]

> ALL IS WELL INDEED BELOVED BON VOYAGE ALL
> LOVE MINUTES COUNT NOW

October 25, 1929

S.S. *Bremen*. Just to mark this hour—1 A.M.—this day to remember forever.

October 28, 1929

At sea now for three days, and all around me is space and time, so different from those last days in New York when there was so much to do, so many people to see.

Luncheon with Miss Seaman was exciting, and into my hands she put the biggest check I have ever seen—One Thousand Dollars—the advance from the Junior Literary Guild. *Harvester* is Bob's story, of course, but the shaping and the research, the typing, presentation to an editor, and the proofreading was my part, and Bob had insisted that I take the first payment; all moneys in the future will go to him. After luncheon I went to the bank to close my account, and there I had some of the money converted into English pounds, some into travelers checks,

108

and some into cash. Then I went to Hattie Carnegie's and bought my wedding dress.

I knew what I wanted and when I saw the dress, I knew it was IT. Moss green, with a wide beige collar, like a fichu, that loops into a soft tie. I'll be able to use it for many occasions. I had never been inside Hattie Carnegie's in my life, but I knew it was a very special place. I had never spent such a sum for a dress, three hundred dollars, but I'll only be married once. I showed it to Bob and he approved. When I showed it to Eunice, she wanted to paint a picture of me in it, but I will not put it on until the very day. What the date will be, I do not know, only that it will be soon. Bill is tending to all those details.

Somehow everything did get done. Then, on that last day, in the early evening, Bob took Sinna and me to the *Bremen* for the sailing at midnight. Sinna was put in the charge of the Dog Steward, my trunk disappeared with dozens of others into the hold, an officer took my ticket, checked my passport, and directed us to my cabin. It was like going into a garden—flowers and flowers, as well as a pile of mail, several telegrams, some packages. People kept appearing at the door and squeezing into the room. I never knew I had so many friends. There were the near and dear ones like Eunice and Gregg and Mrs. Brown, fellow Comparison Shoppers from Macy's, Mrs. Howard from the Frankl Gallery, Mildred Harrington from the *American* with her nice husband, Peter. It seemed as if everyone who had had anything to do with my life during the past three years had come to wish me bon voyage. We talked and laughed and they said all the things said to a traveler, but this was no ordinary trip I was going on and coming back from, this was an extraordinary trip, and there was a fringe of sadness to it.

When gongs started to sound and people were told to be off the ship, good-bys were said in earnest, and one by one my friends left. I went to the railing on the top deck to watch them go down the gangplank and take their places in a crowd of people all smiling and waving; then the gangplank was pulled up, and I could feel the great ship slowly edging away from the dock and into the open sea.

Back in my cabin I was suddenly assailed by loneliness. Here was all the evidence of friendship—flowers, fruit, letters—and here was I, myself, alone. I thought of Sinna asleep in his kennel on the boat deck. I thought of Bill waiting beyond the horizon, and then I thought that I had chosen the way in which I must go, and I got hold of myself.

I am enjoying days of quiet thinking and earnest communion with God. Except for a daily walk with Sinna, when the kennels are opened, and going to the dining salon three times a day, I keep to myself. There are many letters to write, and it's fun to use the S.S. *Bremen* stationery. The letter from Loyola I am copying here so that in the midst of my new life I'll be reminded of my pencil. "My only advice is that you keep at your writing, do something every single day, even if it's only a page or two. I'm still convinced that you will someday make a name for yourself, and I want you to keep plugging till you do, even if success seems a long time in coming. I have positive faith in you, and you will always find me encouraging, as, despite the little success we have had so far, I *know* you have talent."

Among the books given me is Stevenson's *Travels with a Donkey*. I like its gentle pace, and it is a good antidote for the excitement that is rushing through me. I sit for long hours in my deck chair, eyes on the far horizon, and I feel a graver assurance and a deeper faith than ever becoming a part of my being. So much has slipped into the past. I am ready for the future.

I have written a Decalogue before Marriage and will keep it here in my Journal as a reminder.

Evening after evening, while sitting in my deck chair, I see the first star appear—sometimes in a clear sky, sometimes through a tumult of clouds—and I wish on it: to make Bill happy and, for myself, to hold on to happiness no matter what. Stevenson says it for me: "There is no duty we underrate so much as the duty of happiness."

[Radiotelegram from London]

HURRAH SOUTHAMPTON WEDNESDAY ON TENDER EXCITED LOVE

October 30, 1929

In my room at the Cadogan Hotel, London

For five days the horizon was my boundary, then land appeared—a faint line at first, then growing more pronounced and green, so green, on the port side. Land's End. The Cornish coast. Devon. Another hour and houses could be distinguished, then cattle and sheep. By midafternoon, as we came into Southampton Harbor, buildings and wharves seemed very near. The throb of the engines that had been like

111

music for days ceased, and the great ship was no longer cleaving her way through the water but resting in it. Out from the wharves came a small boat moving toward the *Bremen*. There were men in uniform aboard, customs officials, immigration officials in navy dress. Among them was one civilian standing straight and tall, hatless; his dark coat with all the evidence of English tailoring distinguished him from the others in uniform. Dozens of people were leaning against the rail watching the tender as it approached, perhaps wondering who the civilian was who waved his arms.

A ship's officer tapped me on the shoulder and asked me to come below. When the tender touched the *Bremen*, the customs men came aboard through an opening at sea level over a short gangplank. Someone asked to see my passport and stamped it, another said I was to go ashore now, "Captain's orders." With a sailor's arm steadying me I crossed the short distance and was on the tender and Bill's arms were around me. The tender backed away from the *Bremen*, the engine chugged, and Bill and I were headed back to shore in the boat that had held all the officials, alone, save for the sailor at the small engine. What do you say to the man you haven't seen for six months and with whom you are going to spend the rest of your life?

But there were details, there always are, and Bill got through them quickly. Sinna would be met by the carrying agent, my trunk would be passed by the customs and opened in London, because I was coming to take up residence. Mr. Mangum had put his car at Bill's disposal. At the wharf I could see a limousine with a chauffeur standing beside it. As the tender nudged into its berth, we turned to thank the sailor. He gave us a broad smile, touched his cap, and in the first English voice I had heard wished us luck. When we reached the car, the chauffeur murmured a discreet word of welcome as I got in, then the Rolls, purring with a gentler sound than the *Bremen*, took us to the Southampton Hotel.

"Come back in two hours, Pullen," Bill said.

"Very good, sir," Pullen replied.

In the dining room we sat at a small table near a window. There was an electric light with a pink silk shade on the table, and I think I shall see it in my mind always. There was so much we wanted to say to each other, yet somehow nothing mattered for a little while but to look into each other's eyes; and then it was as if there had been no time between, no parting at all.

But we did talk and we did eat.

Bill told me he had received heartening letters from Father and Mother and that all was in order for our wedding a week from today, on November 6, but that I would need a witness to stand up with me. Did I know anyone in England? No one yet, but I would discover someone. Mr. Mangum was loaning us his cottage for the weekend. The furnished flat in Bruton Street was small, but it would do until we found something larger. Bill was eager for my news. Laughter punctuated our talk, and every now and then I reached out to touch his hand, just to assure myself that we were real, that I wasn't in a dream, or pretending.

Then his tone changed, his expression became subdued and, even as his hand rested on mine, he spoke of releasing me. He reminded me of what he

113

had said about his eyes on that mist-shrouded day in the fire tower. "I tried to tell you before, but you wouldn't listen. This time you must listen." I had never seen him so serious.

"Oh, Bill, it doesn't matter."

"It goes back a long way, it could be carried into the future. Look ahead and think of what this may do to your life."

I knew what he meant and I knew that it would not matter. Looking into those gray pools of quiet that were his eyes, I shook my head. There are times when there are no words. There were none for me then.

What I wanted to say was that our marriage—what it would mean to us and might mean, in time, to others—would be the important thing, but the only words I could come out with were those that said I loved him. He smiled, that wonderful smile I had seen so often in memory during the past months, and the pressure of his hand on mine increased. Who knew what the years that stretched ahead might hold, or not hold; we would be traveling them together, strengthening each other, sharing the adventure of life.

Pullen was waiting for us, the door held open. He tucked a lap rug over us as we settled into the backseat, then the car was under way through the streets of Southampton on to the broad road that led to London. It was dark. There were lights in the little towns as we went through them. I held Bill's hand under the lap rug. My head found its place on his shoulder. I knew that I had come home.

It was midnight when Pullen drew up to the Cadogan Hotel. Everything was dark and quiet. A porter came down to take my bag. At the desk Bill was handed a key and was told the room was ready. We went upstairs and Bill seemed to know exactly where to go. When we stood before a door he said, "This is your home in London for a week until you come to 34 Bruton Street"; then he opened the door and we went in. A lamp was on, and what I saw made me wonder if I was a princess in a story. It was a small cozy room, a coal fire was burning cheerily in the grate, there was a table and on it a vase of red roses just opening in the warmth. The bed against one wall had been turned down—linen sheets, and big pillows, and a down comforter. On a stand near the bed was a card in that hand I knew so well with just the word WELCOME. It was so beautiful, so inviting, I'm sure I'll see that room all my life in my mind's eye just as it was at that moment when I stood on the threshold.

November 5, 1929

I've been here almost a week, and London seems so like home I wonder if I have ever lived anyplace else. What a week—so full and yet so different from that last one in New York! I must catch the days up in words now, because after tomorrow I may not write soon again, not because there won't be time but because there won't be need. It will be as if everything had been accomplished. This is the point toward which my life has been tending for the last two and a half years.

We have had breakfast together every morning at the Cadogan, then Bill has gone to his office, and I've had the whole day to myself until we meet for dinner. And I've had much to do. His bachelor flat hardly had enough for even simple housekeeping, so I've been making purchases. I've discovered different stores. As well as buying pots and pans, I've bought some beautiful things, too. Venetia, near Harrod's, had a Venetian amber-glass bowl that will be lovely for fruit or flowers, and to go with it I bought some amber glasses. I cabled a friend in New York who gave me the name of her aunt in Ashtead, Surrey, and when I phoned her and told her of my need for a witness, she invited me to tea. Pullen drove me down and back. My first friend, Mrs. Balmain, will be my ever friend, for we liked each other from the start. She and Mr. Balmain will come to the wedding tomorrow and stand beside me as if they had always known me. They are both quite old, but they made me feel as if I belonged to them.

The days are damp. Twilight begins to settle in at teatime. When we drive through the country, there are still leaves on some of the trees but they are pale gold and russet; the fields are green, and the air has in it the smell of all the coal fires burning for warmth. I like it.

Thanksgiving Day, 1929

34 Bruton Street, London

And now I am Bill's wife.

On the morning of November 6, I dressed in my new green dress with the soft fichu. The porter came for my bag, and I said good-by to the cozy little room that had been my home for a week; then I took a taxi to Bruton Street where Bill was waiting for me. We went to the Piccadilly Hotel for a late breakfast—lamb kidneys and bacon, crisp dry toast, and tea; we might have preferred coffee but have learned that tea is better. It was a gently rainy day, so we didn't walk but took a taxi to Princes-row Registry Office, almost in the shade of Buckingham Palace. Many were there already—Bill's friends, people from his office, and my dear Balmains. Everyone was smiling and happy.

Just at noon—and I could imagine that I heard Big Ben in the distance—we were ushered into a room where an official sat at a desk. He asked for our names and our intent. We were not called upon for vows, only to repeat after him the words:

"I, William, take you, Elizabeth, for my lawful wedded wife."

"I, Elizabeth, take you, William, for my lawful wedded husband."

The ring of glorious sincerity in Bill's voice was thrilling. We signed some papers, and that was all. Such a chorus of good wishes, such handshaking, and most of them from people I'd never seen before. The embrace that mattered most was back at Bruton Street where we went to change into our country clothes. "All of me to you, darling, forever," Bill said when he put his arms around me.

Pullen arrived to drive us down to the Mangums' cottage at Ferring-by-the-Sea, but first he took us to the Royal Court Hotel in Sloane Square, where we had a festive luncheon. On the way out of London we stopped to send cables to my mother and father, and to Bill's mother, then we were off. The drive over quiet roads through a muted countryside, with twilight coming through the rain, was a rare experience. Everything seemed so gentle.

117

It was dusk when we arrived at Bay Tree Cottage, a small, thatched fourteenth-century dwelling. There was a light glowing within and a little old woman opened the door to us. "I've put a chicken in the oven for you," she said, "and you'll find other things. What a pile of telegrams you've got! I'll be back in the morning to do for you." She scuttled off into the mist, and Pullen was soon on the road back to London, not to return for us until Sunday afternoon.

There we were with each other, a crackling coal fire making an area of warmth, and a delicious aroma coming from the oven; and there was that stack of telegrams to open. One of them, from Bill's office manager in Scotland, "Lang may your lum reek," had to be translated for me, "Long may your chimney smoke." The one from Dublin was quite clear, "May a wee moose ne'er leave your hoose."

There is so much that I will remember always, but as my inner eye will see things, my inner ear will hear Bill's voice saying "Good night, my wife." There was a solemnity and beauty in his tone that thrilled me, as his promise had in the Registry Office earlier that day.

And it was all real, for the next day in the *London Times* was the statement:

Mr. W. J. McGreal and Miss M. E. Yates

Mr. William James McGreal of Rochester, New York, and Miss Mary Elizabeth Yates of Buffalo, New York, were married on November 6, at noon, at the Princes-row Registry Office, London, S.W., in the presence of a representative from the American Consulate-General and a large body of friends.

Thursday, Friday, Saturday, and most of Sunday we walked—on the pebbly beach with the sea rolling in at our feet, up on the Downs were the wind was sharp, to the next village with tea at the local pub. But, because the days drew in early, we were soon back at the cottage, with a fire burning, a lamp glowing, and a meal that the little old lady had prepared for us. And we talked—sharing ideas, making plans, reading about England and English ways. Bill had an advantage over me, as he had already been there for six months, but I had memories of my time in "the old country" when I was eighteen. Whatever discussions we started on—philosophical or practical, business or literary—there was the marvelous feeling that we could continue it on the next day, or the next; a lifetime of days stretched before us.

On Sunday afternoon Pullen came precisely at five, "so you would have had your tea," he said. Then we were on the way back to London.

On Monday morning we had an early breakfast at Slater's. Bill always wanted to be at the office an hour before anyone else arrived to get things ready for the day. When he left I watched him go down the street to the big red bus that would take him to Holborn. Suddenly I had an utterly blank feeling. An aloneness more total than any I had ever known before swept over me. I sat on at the table and had a conversation with myself. In the midst of so much happiness, with a peace of heart that went beyond my dreams, I seemed compelled to face the thought of death. This was not something I could talk about with Bill. It was a personal problem to which I would have to find my answer. Should I die, it would be simple—a new adventure, a new dimension, the existence of which I had no doubt. If Bill should die, what would happen to me? I faced the stark possibility and told myself that I would go on with life. It would still be our life until the end came for me and I would catch up with Bill, wherever he was, whatever doing.

Now, three weeks later, I can say that we have moved into a smooth pattern of living. The hours with Bill are serene and happy, the hours alone are rich and stimulating; and just to be a part of the life of London is magnificent. Did anyone, anywhere, ever have such an overflowing cup as I on this Thanksgiving Day?